FAITH THAT OVERCOMES THE WORLD

Ulf Ekman

Ulf Ekman Ministries
www.ulfekman.org

FAITH THAT OVERCOMES THE WORLD
Sixth edition, 2nd print, 2003

ISBN 91 7866 404 7

Cover design, Gustav Magnusson
Cover picture, Sjöbergs Bildbyrå

Printed in Finland by WS Bookwell, Finland 2003

Acknowledgments
Unless otherwise indicated, Scripture quotations are
from the *New King James Version* of the Bible, copyright
© 1979, 1980, 1982 Thomas Nelson Publishers, Inc. Used
by permission

Scripture quotations noted NIV are from the *Holy Bible, New
International Version,* copyright © 1973, 1978, 1984 International
Bible Society; those noted AMP are from the Amplified Bible. Used
by permission of Zondervan Bible Publishers.

Table of Contents

Foreword

For your growth in faith, I recommend Ulf Ekman's book *Faith that Overcomes the World*.

A spiritual leader for many areas of Northern Europe, Ulf Ekman expounds the truth: that God has given every believer a measure of faith, which increases through one's personal study of the Word of God.

Our generation needs clear-cut teaching regarding faith in action. It is faith that achieves. It is faith to live by.

Ulf Ekman shows us faith which functions through prayer. His teaching on faith being related to financial prosperity is Biblical and experiential.

Lester Sumrall
South Bend, Indiana, USA

Introduction

Faith that Overcomes the World introduces you to faith that works in practice.

There is nothing impractical or unrealistic about the New Testament principles of faith. They produce positive results in the life of the believer.

By learning to live according to the Biblical principles Ulf Ekman expounds, you can have a faith that overcomes, no matter what the circumstances of your life.

Colin Urquhart
Horsham, England

Preface

God is a good God. He has revealed His love and His will for us through His Son, Jesus Christ. When we look at Jesus, we see God's nature, God's ability, and God's will.

Today the Holy Spirit is in the process of revealing the Word of God, the Bible, to all those who seek God with an honest heart. Revelation knowledge is flowing forth and believers are beginning to see who they really are in Christ.

We are beginning to comprehend just how much we have in Christ and what we are able to do through Him. Believers are rising up and shaking off every chain of ignorance and every misconception about God that the devil has used to keep them in bondage. The Bible is becoming clear and understandable once again. The Christian life is becoming concrete and attractive.

Jesus and His victory are becoming living realities in the everyday life of the believer. The Holy Spirit is showing us what it really means to walk in faith; and that through faith in Jesus we have victory available to us in every area of our lives. What Jesus accomplished at Calvary is becoming a manifest reality which is changing thousands of lives. The preaching of the Cross is once again the real, life-changing power of God. Believers are realising that the Living God, the God we serve, actually does work miracles just as He promised. These are the times we are living in.

By the Word and the Spirit, a restoration of apostolic power and revelation is washing over the world today, like a wave. It is a truly exciting time we are living in just now! God is working miracles, revealing His true nature, and filling the whole earth with His glory. Blessed be His Holy name! Jesus is truly Lord!

Ulf Ekman

1

The God of Faith

For whatever is born of God overcomes the world. And this is the victory that has overcome the world—our faith. Who is he who overcomes the world, but he who believes that Jesus is the Son of God? (1 John 5:4-5).

Faith is just a short word, but what it contains is revolutionary. It takes a lifetime and more to understand its real meaning and an eternity to live it out. The Bible is full of faith—from Genesis to Revelation. Faith is something which pleases God, but something the devil hates and resists.

God's people are called to live by faith, and when its nature and essence are revealed and begin to operate in their lives, they will never be the same again.

A whole new world opens up to them. Heaven kisses earth and God is made visible. Jesus said,

Did I not say to you that if you would believe you would see the glory of God? (John 11:40).

Before we discover what faith is, it is important to understand that we are talking about faith in God. We are *not* talking about faith in ourselves or our own ability, nor do we mean faith in our mind, will, or emotions. We are talking about faith in God and His ability; a faith which centres around God Himself.

The world likes to talk about faith, but means something entirely different to the Biblical definition of the word. To the world, faith is nothing more than a loose assumption like, "I believe the weather will be nice tomorrow! But I'm not too sure." Or, "I believe in the future", in other words, "I hope everything works out all right, and that's why I can be somewhat optimistic." This may be the world's concept of faith, but it has nothing to do with true Biblical faith. Faith is *not* merely thinking positively, in other words trying to convince yourself that things will eventually improve.

Have the Faith of God

So what exactly is faith? To find out, we need to know the source of faith Himself—God! Jesus said to His disciples in Mark 11:22, *Have faith in God.* This may also be translated, "Have the faith of God," or "Have the faith that God has." God is the source of faith and all faith comes directly from Him. He Himself has faith and from out of His faith we receive our faith. When this begins to work in our lives it produces supernatural results.

So what is faith? Hebrews 11:1 (AMP) says, *Now faith is assurance of the things we hope for, being the proof of things we do not see and the conviction of their reality.*

Faith is not a loose assumption or something about which we are not sure.

Faith is a conviction and an assurance

Faith is not having a generally optimistic attitude about something you are hoping will work out.

Faith is an absolute conviction. It is something about which you are fully convinced and from which you cannot be moved, no matter how things around you may appear. Your circumstances may be completely contradictory, but faith is a conviction about things we *do not* see.

This is the kind of faith Jesus talks about in Mark 11:23-24 when He says, *For assuredly, I say to you, whoever says to this mountain, "Be removed and be cast into the sea," and does not doubt in his heart, but believes that those things he says will come to pass, he will have whatever he says.*

This kind of faith produces supernatural results. This is the kind of faith that does not shrink back from insurmountable odds, but sees what God can do instead. It is convinced about things which cannot be seen and even causes great mountains to move. Jesus calls it *faith of the heart,* a faith which obtains the promises of God.

For with the heart one believes to righteousness, and with the mouth confession is made to salvation (Romans 10:10).

It is this heartfelt faith which produces eternal life in you, changes your circumstances, moves mountains and brings you answers to prayer. What Jesus said in Matthew 21:22 becomes a reality, *And all things, whatever you ask in prayer, believing, you will receive.* Jesus says that the faith which comes from our hearts is a conviction, not just a vague assumption, and it is this kind of faith that receives whatever it asks for.

Now if this is what faith can produce, and if Satan is our adversary in this world, it is not so strange that he attacks faith and the teaching of faith. He is the enemy of faith and is opposed to any sort of divine intervention in this world. When you receive an answer to prayer, God is glorified. When you receive an answer to prayer, His presence is made manifest in your life for others to see. Satan attacks your faith because he does not want the presence of God to be manifested.

Faith Puts Satan on the Run

James 4:7 says, *Resist the devil and he will flee from you*. In what way are you to resist him?

1 Peter 5:9 says, *Resist him, steadfast in the faith*. In other words, by faith we can put the devil on the run and get him to flee from us.

Ephesians 6:16 says, *Above all, taking the shield of faith with which you **will be able** to quench all the fiery darts of the wicked one.*

If your shield of faith can quench *all* the fiery darts of the wicked one, no wonder he wants to take it away from you. Without the shield of faith, his darts cannot be quenched. No wonder the devil resists, backbites, lies and frightens people as he attempts to stop them from becoming grounded and established in the faith. For as soon as faith becomes a steadfast conviction in your heart, he will have to flee—and he knows that. That is why he wants to keep *you* from knowing this.

Faith, then, is a heartfelt belief in God and faith comes from God. That is why it is impossible to have faith in God without knowing who he is. Faith trusts in God, relies on Him, and expects every good thing from Him. But if I do not know who God is or how He thinks and acts, I will not know what to expect from Him.

Hebrews 11:6 says, *But without faith it is impossible to please Him, for he who comes to God must believe that He is, and that He is a rewarder of those who diligently seek Him.*

Believing is the way to please God. When I come to Him I must first believe that He exists. This may seem obvious, but these words also have a deeper meaning. God's name is *I AM* (Exodus 3:14), and He wants to reveal to you not only *that* He is, but also *who* He is.

When you know who God is—His personality and character, what pleases Him, what He does, and what He wants—then you are able to approach Him in faith. Then you are able to approach Him steadfast and with conviction. With what kind of conviction? That *He is a rewarder of those who diligently seek Him.* God wants us to know that when we come to Him, He is ready to reward and answer us, help us and lead us. God is not pleased when we come to Him without expecting anything. It does not please Him when we come feeling unsure of His character and of how He might respond. He wants us to come with a firm conviction, in other words with a knowledge of *who* He is and *what* He will do. You can only do that through fellowship with Him and getting to know Him intimately.

For many people, God is nothing more than an abstract concept. He is so awe-inspiring that they hardly dare approach Him, even less think of troubling Him with their trivial problems.

For others, God is so huge, inscrutable, and remote, so elevated above day-to-day life that the idea of coming to Him with their daily cares is completely alien to them.

God has often been described as something so incomprehensible that understanding His thoughts and His will has seemed impossible.

Religious traditions have described God in such a way as to totally obscure His nature and will.

But God is not like that. He is our Father, He is available to us, and His will has been revealed to us.

God is a Good Father

Hebrews 4:16 says, *Let us therefore come boldly to the throne of grace, that we may obtain mercy and find grace to help in time of need.* God wants you to come to Him boldly in order to receive all the help you need.

The devil has forever tried to give people the wrong image of God, so that He appears to be some kind of monster who strikes blindly and madly at everything in sight. Like some kind of universal policeman, He is always in a bad mood, ready to repress and subdue all those who dare to raise their head.

Our relationship with Him has been distorted to be more like a courtroom appearance rather than spending time with family. We have shown up only when our conscience has bothered us, and have felt inferior and miserable while with Him. We have confessed our sins and received forgiveness, then breathed a sigh of relief as we darted away from His presence to escape our discomfort.

But God is our Heavenly Father, and He wants to have fellowship with us. He wants to love us, teach us, guide us, instruct us, and use us in a variety of ways. He cannot do this though, if the image we have of Him scares us away from Him.

The devil is well aware of this fact. And for that reason he has tried to plant in us a picture of God where we blame Him for everything that goes wrong in our lives, and we become bitter, and eventually stop having fellowship with Him altogether.

If you blame your Father for everything that happens when He is not the guilty party, you will have problems relating to Him. You will be unable to come to Him in faith and expect Him to hear you. This is Satan's aim. He wants to destroy your communion with God and prevent His power from flowing through you and out to the world.

This is why you must become acquainted with your Father.

Let no one say when he is tempted, "I am tempted by God"; for God cannot be tempted by evil, nor does He Himself tempt anyone. But each one is tempted when he is drawn away by his own desires and enticed. Then, when desire has conceived, it gives birth to sin; and sin, when it is full-grown, brings forth death. Do not be deceived, my beloved brethren. Every good gift and every perfect gift is from above, and comes down from the Father of lights, with whom there is no variation or shadow of turning (James 1:13-17).

What is the Holy Spirit telling us in this passage from James' letter? He is saying, do not go astray—do not let yourself be deceived! Call to mind what comes from God and what does not!

Every good and perfect gift comes from God. If it is not good and perfect then it does not come from God. God does not change;

He is light and in Him there is no darkness (1 John 1:5). He is good and every good thing comes from Him.

Jesus said in John 10:10, *The thief does not come except to steal, and to kill, and to destroy. I have come that they may have **life**, and that they may have it **more abundantly**.* This is God's nature: He gives His best to us, and His plans and will for us are always His very best.

If you want to know what God is like and be able to understand His will; look at Jesus. Do not look at an isolated piece of Scripture in the Old Testament; look at Jesus.

Jesus reveals God's will to us. Hebrews 1:3 tells us that Jesus is *the brightness of His glory and **the express image of His person**.* Hebrews 10:7 says, *Behold, I have come—in the volume of the book it is written of Me—to do Your will, O God.*

The Word and the Spirit Reveal God's Will

Jesus came to do God's will and He was the express image of God.

Everything Jesus says is what the Father says, and everything Jesus does is what the Father does. Jesus was never out of the will of God—not even for a second. Everything He said and did was exactly what the Father wanted Him to say and do.

In John 5:19 Jesus says,

The Son can do nothing of Himself, but what He sees the Father do; for whatever He does, the Son also does in like manner.

The Son followed the Father and did what His Father did.

So, when you see Jesus preach, teach, forgive sins, heal the sick, and cast out devils, you can be assured that this is the Father's will, since He came to reveal the Father and His will for us. Just as Jesus is, so is your Father. God never changes.

13

Jesus is the Word and God reveals Himself in His Word, the Bible. God is not the Bible, but the Bible was inspired by Him and is the divine revelation of His will. The Bible is His covenant, or in other words, His Last Will and Testament. He has filled the Bible—the Word—with His promises to let you know His nature and will. He has not kept His will concealed from you, instead He has revealed it to you, so that you shall see it and know it.

1 Corinthians 2:9-10 and 12 tells us that God has prepared things for those who love Him and that these things have been revealed to us by His Spirit. We have received His Spirit, not the spirit of the world, in order that *we might know what* God has freely given us.

God is not hidden from us. He has not hidden His will from us to make us confused every time something happens. God has revealed Himself and His will to us so we can feel secure and at rest in Him as we watch His plans come to pass in our lives.

How has He made Himself known? By His Spirit and through His Word. God's Word is the revelation of His will. God is *greater* than the Bible, but He is completely *consistent* with the Bible. He is not such that He says one thing in the Bible and then goes away and does something completely different. He has committed Himself to His Covenant Word; He has promised to do what He has said.

Because of this, we should not merely blame everything on God. Instead, we must find out what He has actually said and promised. We need to recognise what comes from God and what does not, so we can *receive* what comes from Him by faith and, in faith steadfastly *resist* what does not come from Him.

That is why James says in his epistle, *Do not be deceived, my beloved brethren. Every good gift and every perfect gift is from above, and comes down from the Father of lights, with whom there is no variation or shadow of turning* (James 1:16-17).

God is a good God and He has revealed His good will to you because He loves you. His Word is His will and He wants you to believe in Him, expect every good thing from Him, be convinced that what He says is true, and that what He has promised will come to pass.

God Himself is full of faith. He wants us to have faith of the heart, but He too has faith. Long ago He planned the universe. He believed that it would come into existence. He had planned it and meditated on it until His heart was full of it. Then when His heart was full, He spoke—for out of the abundance of the heart the mouth speaks. When God spoke, creative power was released. What He had seen in His heart and the things He was convinced of—even if He had not seen them—came into being through the power released in His Word. Through His faith the world came into existence, both the visible and the invisible.

This same faith, which is able to accomplish such great things, has been given by God to every believer.

God Has Given His Faith to You— both in Quantity and in Quality

Romans 12:3 says that *God has dealt to each one the measure of faith.*

Faith comes from God. It is not of human origin, it is *supernatural*. It is a part of God's nature and is called faith of the heart. This faith is produced by God Himself and is given to every believer. When you are born again, the Spirit of God comes to recreate you and dwell within you. The old man dies, a new man is created, and you become a new creation in Christ Jesus (2 Corinthians 5:17).

The Bible says that since you were created in His image, like God, you are triune. You are spirit, soul, and body (1 Thessalonians 5:23). The Bible sometimes refers to your spirit as your heart, so when you are born again, you receive a new heart. A new man is created within you and your spirit is made new.

In your spirit, or heart, God puts a measure of faith. He does not put it in your understanding, He puts it in your heart. For this reason, it is called faith of the heart. This faith came into you along with the Holy Spirit at the new birth. In 2 Corinthians 4:13 the Holy Spirit is called the Spirit of faith.

What is this measure of faith that God has given you? We can look at faith both in terms of quantity and quality.

Quantitatively—how much faith has God given you? God always gives in abundance, giving you everything you need and more besides.

1 Corinthians 10:13 says,

No temptation has overtaken you except such as is common to man; but God is faithful, who will not allow you to be tempted beyond what you are able, but with the temptation will also make the way of escape that you may be able to bear it.

Paul is saying that you will never be tempted, tried or attacked beyond *your ability* to resist. What is your ability? In ourselves we can do nothing, but *all things are possible to him who believes* (Mark 9:23). So, the faith that God has given you is your ability. You have received a measure of faith which has the potential to do all things. That is why 1 John 5:4 says, *For whatever is born of God overcomes the world...*

Now, this is the *quality* of faith. Since faith is not a human invention, but has divine, supernatural qualities, it can accomplish anything when it is released. Though it be as small as a grain of mustard seed, the smallest of all seeds, it has the quality and ability to do the impossible. Why? Because it comes from God and *with God nothing will be impossible* (Luke 1:37).

In Matthew 17:20 Jesus says,

If you have faith as a mustard seed, you will say to this mountain, 'Move from here to there,' and it will move; and nothing will be impossible for you.

That was what Jesus said to His disciples about faith before they had been born again; even before the Holy Spirit had come.

We have been born again; we have the Spirit of God. The Holy Spirit is the Spirit of faith. God has given you a measure of His own faith. That faith is the faith of the heart and it produces supernatural results. Yes, even if it is as small as a grain of mustard seed it can move mountains. So you do not need to measure your faith or the faith of others. Do not do that. Instead, all you need to know is that as a believer you have faith, and the measure you have received is sufficient. Now all you need is to get this measure to work for you.

When you hear teaching about faith, the devil wants to distort what you hear about it and bring condemnation into your life. Of a certainty, he wants to tell you that you do not have any faith and that therefore God cannot hear you, and He does not want to answer your prayers. That is all lies. If you are a believer and have been born again, you have faith. All believers have faith. You have received a measure of faith. It might not always be active and in operation, but it is there, nonetheless. If you are a believer, then you have faith.

Faith is Active where the Will of God is Known

When Paul wrote to the various churches, he never prayed that they would get faith. Instead, he gave thanks that they were believers and already had faith. What he prayed was that they would receive knowledge, as in Ephesians 1:15-19. Why? Because he knew that faith is made active through the knowledge of God's will. Faith is active only where the will of God is known. In the sixth verse of the epistle to Philemon, Paul prays this type of prayer, *That the sharing*

17

of your faith may become effective by the acknowledgement of every good thing which is in you in Christ Jesus.

Paul does not pray for Philemon to get faith—he tells him he already has faith. Why? Because God has given to *everybody* a measure of faith. However, this faith can be either effective or ineffective, active or passive. And Paul prays that it shall become effective, so that it begins to produce results. And how will faith become effective? Through insight. Through knowledge. Through the Word!

This is why in Ephesians 1:17-19, Paul prays for those who are already believers to receive *the spirit of wisdom and revelation in the knowledge of Him.* In the knowledge of whom? God, the Father of glory! And in the knowledge of what? *Every good thing which is in you in Christ Jesus* (Philemon 6). When you realise just how many good things you have in Christ, then will your faith become effective. And what brings this realisation? Knowledge of the Word of God.

In Romans 12:3 Paul speaks about the measure of faith. It can be compared to a measure of seed or grain. When you activate your faith, you take from the faith you have been given and sow into any one of a number of fields which correspond to the various needs and circumstances in your life. Where you have sown, you will reap; and what is harvested is always more than was sown. This is the way your faith will increase, so that what seems hopeless and fruitless at first will gradually become more and more effective. But remember, even though God has given you the seed, you have the responsibility to sow it and put it to use.

Your faith will become active and effective only as you put it to use. Though it may seem small and insignificant compared to the circumstances, the mountains and difficulties in your life, Jesus has promised that faith produces supernatural results.

However small it may seem, faith always looks to God, and God is greater than any and every possible circumstance.

2

Faith Comes by the Word of God

In the previous chapter we said that faith comes from God and that every believer has received a measure of faith. Yet there are times when this faith does not seem to work. When things go wrong in our Christian life we are often quick to blame our circumstances or even God. But this is a wrong attitude which goes back as far as Adam. Following his sin, he excused himself by saying, *The woman whom You gave to be with me, she gave me of the tree, and I ate* (Genesis 3:12).

This is one of our most common mistakes. When things go wrong, we blame our circumstances, and often God Himself. So God is given the blame for something He never did. We might say something that He chose not to answer our prayer, without checking to see if what we prayed for was in line with His Word.

When we pray, we should pray in faith, and faith is only effective when the will of God is known. When the will of God is known, faith will not be a problem.

God is Not the Problem—He is the Solution

We have to come away from our often unconscious idea that God is our problem. God is not our problem; He is the *solution* to all our problems.

If your radio is not working, you do not call the radio station and get upset with them. You simply adjust the frequency of your receiver. If that does not help, you get it repaired by someone who knows how to fix it. The same is true of God. If something is not working properly, do not blame it on God. There is nothing wrong with the transmitter—it is the receiver that needs adjusting. This is where we opened the way for both rebellion and condemnation.

Rebellion is the result of not wanting to submit to the Word of God. For this reason we think that we have a lot of good reasons, experiences, and circumstances which excuse us from having to obey God's Word. "Surely there must be some exception or an easier way just for me," we say. We are like the people who try to push their way past the line in the post office, thinking they are the only ones who can justify being in a hurry. They might even get upset if they fail to get their way.

This sort of behaviour is extremely selfish. The Bible says that God is no respecter of persons, meaning He treats every one of us the same; and He treats us well because He loves us. If He has said something in His Word, He will not make a special exception just for you. Instead, He will give you all the help He has to offer so that His promises can be fulfilled in your life. The only prerequisite is that you submit to and obey His Word.

In James 1:5-8 the Lord says that if you lack wisdom (and this applies to every area of your life), you are to ask for it and you will receive it. *But* when you pray, you must pray believing, without doubting. *For he who doubts is like a wave of the sea driven and tossed by the wind.* Regarding a wavering person the Lord says, **let not that man suppose that he will receive anything from the Lord.**

This is where condemnation usually begins, and because we feel condemned, we either try to explain this sort of Scripture away or just ignore it altogether. But that will not help you. First of all, we have to acknowledge that God is the one who actually said this. It

20

was not just James or some fanatical preacher. No, the Holy Spirit has inspired this Scripture, and if God has said it, it is the truth and we need to submit to it.

But He did not say this to beat you over the head or put you down and condemn you. He is not in the business of condemning people. God loves you, He is for you, He is with you, and He wants to help you. He has given you these words to encourage, strengthen, and correct you, so that you will be open and always ready to receive from Him.

And how do you receive from God? By faith! How did you get saved? By faith! Not only were you saved by faith; as a Christian your whole life is to be one *of* faith. Romans 1:17 says, *The just shall live by faith*. The whole of the rest of your life—not just the moment when you were born again—has to be a walk in and of faith.

Romans 14:23 states, *whatever is not from faith is sin*. What does that mean? It means God wants your whole life and all that you do to be impregnated with faith; faith which is the knowledge, trust and security that God is who He says He is and always does what He has promised to do.

Get to Know God's Character and Will Through His Word
When we understand that what God says is always motivated by love and nothing else, it will be easier for us to receive from Him. Then, we will not fall into condemnation.

Condemnation often comes because we have not listened to *all* that God has said, or because we allow the devil to distort what we have heard. The devil loves to distort and twist what God has said and use it as an accusation instead. He is the Accuser of our brethren (Revelation 12:10), and an expert at accusation and condemnation. He will gladly use the Word against you if he can, but he is only able to do this if you are not established in God's Word or not secure in His loving character.

When you understand God's character and His Word, you can resist the devil and his accusations. Then you will know that what God says is not to reject and condemn you, but to edify and improve. So in James 1:5-8, when God says the one who wavers should not expect to receive anything from Him, it is not to condemn you, but to *help you* to believe that you will be able to receive from Him.

When you have received, you need to be able to hold on to what you have obtained without having it stolen from you.

God's motive is always to do you good, so do not let the devil oppress or condemn you! Jesus often exhorted his disciples to have faith and not doubt (Mark 4:40). This does not mean He thought they were no longer His disciples if they doubted. If your radio does not work, it does not cease to be a radio; it just needs a little adjusting. When a child stumbles in its first steps, it does not lie down and angrily refuse ever to walk again.

The same is true of your walk of faith. God encourages you to keep on going and keep on growing. He does not complain or threaten you. He will not condemn or blame you for lacking faith but will encourage you to grow instead.

There are passages of Scripture in which Jesus seriously rebukes people for their unbelief, but in most cases they were obstinate Pharisees who refused to submit to the Word of God. This is the kind of hardness of heart and unbelief, which exchanges the commandments of God for the traditions of men (Mark 7:6-7), which attacks and denies the Word, which despises miracles and the supernatural, and which resists the work of the Holy Spirit. They have a form of godliness but completely deny its power (2 Timothy 3:5). This kind of pride and rebellion shows open contempt for God. It is sin and it brings only misery.

Jesus strongly opposed the Pharisees, but to His disciples who wanted to follow Him but often understood little of the depth of what He was doing, He showed patience, always teaching and encouraging them.

Often people wonder whether or not they have faith or if they have enough faith, and so the focus of their attention gets taken off the object of faith Himself—God. So it is important to see how faith comes and grows strong.

The Devil Will Always Attack the Word

Romans 10:17 says that *faith comes by hearing, and hearing by the Word of God.* Faith rises by the Word. The Word is the will of God. When the will of God is known, faith is no problem. Problems arise only when we are unaware of or choose not to obey what the Word says.

The devil has always attacked the Word so as to keep people away from God. The first thing we learn about him, in Genesis 3:1, is that he sows doubt in the Word of God; *Has God indeed said...?* And he did not stop there. He has not changed. He is always trying to get you to doubt God's Word. Why? Because God has deposited His life, nature, and power in *His exceedingly great and precious promises, that through these you may be partakers of the divine nature, having escaped the corruption that is in the world through lust* (2 Peter 1:4).

The devil does not want you to escape the corruption that holds sway in the world. He does not want you to be a partaker of the divine nature, to grow and be strong in spirit, or to be free and walk in victory.

So he attacks the Word more than anything else. He knows that the Word will produce faith in your life and that faith produces supernatural results. He knows that when you begin to act on the Word of God, you have taken up the sword of the Spirit, and you will defeat him in one area after another. As a result, he does everything he can to turn the mighty and reliable Word of the Living God into a fairy tale, into something far too simple to be taken literally. Our salvation, however, is in believing what the Word says, doing what it says, for then it *becomes* what it says!

The Word of God is the expression of God's nature. He is exactly as His Word says He is. The same is also true of you and me. What we are is determined by our words. If your words cannot be trusted, neither can you. You are no better than your words. And God is no different. God is eternal. His words are eternal. Matthew 24:35 says, *Heaven and earth will pass away, but My words will by no means pass away.*

God is Spirit. His words are spirit and life (John 4:24; 6:63). God is truth. His words are true (Numbers 23:19). God is a Covenant God. His words are covenant words which He cannot and will not break, since He has sworn and chosen to make a covenant with us based on His promises (Psalms 89:34; Exodus 2:24). God is the Creator. His words are filled with creative power (Genesis 1:3).

It is immensely important for you to understand that God and His Word are inseparable. You cannot say, "I believe in Jesus, but not in the Bible." In John 14:23, Jesus said, *If anyone loves Me, he will keep My word,* meaning that if we do not love Jesus, then we do care about what the Word says. Instead, we will be disobedient and spend our time explaining away everything He said.

In 1 Peter 1:23, the Word of God is called an incorruptible seed. The Word is like seed or grain that cannot go bad. It is eternal and therefore produces eternal results. In just the same way as a seed produces, the Word will produce in your life.

The Word is a Seed Which Produces Supernatural Results
In Mark 4, Jesus tells a parable that is so significant He says,

Do you not understand this parable? How then will you understand all the parables? (Mark 4:13).

This parable is the prerequisite for all that Jesus teaches. Here, He is telling us that the Word is a seed, and reveals to us a fundamental principle which applies to everything in God's Kingdom. It is important that we see the Word of God in this light. When God created the heavens and the earth, He did it with His Word (Genesis 1:3). Hebrews 1:3 says that Jesus upholds all things by the Word of His power. He upholds the entire universe with His Word and the entire universe is held together and ruled by spirit-filled words of creative, miracle-working power. The same words have now become the personal promises you see before you in the Bible.

These words Jesus called seeds and they are able to produce supernatural results in your life. No wonder the devil wants to steal the Word and make you doubt or neglect the Bible!

In Mark 4:10-20, Jesus explains the parable of the sower. He says what the sower sows is the Word—God's Word. The various types of soil represent people's hearts and attitudes, and that the final aim is a harvest. With the right kind of soil the Word will always produce results, so where does the problem lie? Could it be with the seed or the sower? No, the problem is in the soil!

God is never our problem. He is always our solution!

Satan comes immediately to take the Word from the first type of soil, which is by the wayside (v 15). Luke 8:12 says he does this *Lest they should believe and be saved*. The devil knows that the Word will produce faith as soon as it is sown. The Word of God has the capacity within it to produce faith in people's hearts. Faith of the heart comes by the Word. In this case, however, the ground was hard and unprepared, so it easy for the birds to steal the seed.

If we do not allow the Holy Spirit to make our hearts humble and ready to hear and obey God's Word on God's terms, His Word cannot produce faith. We have skeptics and observers who attend many of our meetings. They have not come to be blessed and edified or to seek the face of God—they have come to criticise, control, and give bad reports. They are destined for tragedy. They might sit right next to someone who is absorbing the Word and hearing from God, someone who leaves the meeting built up, blessed, and having received a miracle from the Lord. But the critic hardens his heart, so that the same Word which produces supernatural results in the person sitting next to him produces absolutely nothing in his own life. The birds came immediately and stole it. Why? Because the hardness of the soil (his heart) allowed it. It is not that God wants this to happen, it is that their pride makes it possible.

The next type of soil is the stony ground (v 16). This represents the people who love the preaching and teaching, and not least, after the meeting, when God performs signs and wonders. They receive the Word with gladness, but it does not take root within them on account of the stones and the thin covering of topsoil. So, what's implied here? It means for these people that so long as they are in a meeting where the Spirit of God is present and there is an atmosphere of faith, then they are full of enthusiasm. But then comes a regular workday, and with it the attacks. And they are not prepared for the challenges of everyday life and the affliction and persecution which arises for the sake of the Word (v 17).

The Bible talks about affliction and suffering from which we have been delivered through the suffering of Jesus, as well as affliction and suffering from which we have not been delivered. The latter includes persecution for the sake of the Word.

The devil hates the Word and does not want to see it established in people's lives. So, he does whatever he can to put pressure on you and get you to let go of the Word. How does he do that? One of his tactics is to lie and distort the truth to try to create fear in you. Fear and faith are opposites (Mark 4:40). Faith casts out fear.

Fear casts out faith. The fear of opposition will cast out the Word and prevent it from bringing forth supernatural results in your life.

The devil uses unsaved people and unestablished, compromising Christians to scare and discourage you, give you the wrong information, and make you "come down to earth again". As you begin to act on the Word, you will find yourself in conflict with the world's way of thinking and acting. This is unavoidable. While the world is worrying, you are not, because you have cast all your cares on the Lord. When you are accused of being irresponsible, you will have to choose either to follow men or the Word.

When you have prayed and received your answer by faith in the Word, the circumstances may appear to be seven times worse than before. As the prince of this world, the devil is able to manipulate the circumstances to make it *look as though* your answer will never come. These circumstances are really just persecution because of the Word that has been sown in your heart. If you have any "stony ground" in your life, such as unforgiveness, bitterness, disappointment, unconfessed sin, pride, hatred, anger, and so on, it will come out when you are under attack.

Though everything may seem just fine in a meeting, it is usually in the midst of attacks that the rubble turns up. If you do not get rid of it at that point it will cause you to fall. Then people will undoubtedly wonder, "He seemed so joyful, so full of faith, how could he fall like that?" The reason is because the stones were not removed or the price of following God at the expense of other people's favour seemed too high.

The third type of soil contains thorns (v 18). This type of person also receives the Word, but the problems and cares of daily life are allowed to choke it out completely. Their mental attitude toward the Word is usually, "Of course, I believe the Bible," but the Word does not have first place in their lives. They make no room for reading, studying, meditating, confessing, and praying the

27

Word on an everyday basis. There always seems to be so many other things which keep them busy.

"When I get a bit of spare time, I'll read the Bible", they say, but the time never comes. There are always other things which seem more urgent and important. The Word is choked; though they hear it, it bears no fruit.

The last type of soil, found in verse 20, is the good ground. What type of person does this represent? Like the others he too hears the Word, but unlike the others, he takes enough time in the Word to "understand it" (Matthew 13:23), so that he can truly receive it and keep it with patience (Luke 8:15).

The Word of God has within itself the ability to produce results. You are not the one who produces them. Your part is to allow the Word to be sown in your heart, look after it and hold on to it, even while you are under pressure and in conflicting circumstances. As a result the Word *will* produce in your life. How much? Mark 4:20 says, *some thirtyfold, some sixty, and some a hundred*. Much more than you can comprehend!

When will the harvest come? In verses 26-28 Jesus says, *The kingdom of God is as if a man should scatter seed on the ground, and should sleep* **by night** *and rise* **by day**, *and the seed should sprout and grow, he himself does not know* **how**. *For the earth yields crops* **by itself**: *first the blade, then the head,* **after that** *the full grain in the head*. We always want to know *when* and *how*; but it is not always that we can know when or how. Even Jesus says that the sower does not know *how* it happens. You do not always need to know *how* it happens, only that it *will*!

A seed does not produce results when you put it under a microscope and critically examine every detail of it, but it does when you plant it in the ground! God has not called you to dissect other people's opinions, thoughts, and doctrines, but to sow His Word in your own field and reap a supernatural harvest.

Faith and Patience Bring You the Promises

We usually want to know *when* our answer will come. We want our miracle *now*! But no farmer ever thinks that way. We would laugh if a farmer went out to sow one day and sat down and cried the next because "nothing has happened." Jesus said that nights and days would pass before there would finally be a full corn in the ear.

Hebrews 6:12 says that through faith and *patience* we will inherit the promises. We often forget that there is an element of time involved in receiving a miracle.

So what should we do in the meantime? We should sow the incorruptible seed in every area of our lives.

If I have a need in one particular area, then I have a 'field' into which I can and should be sowing. There is no use wondering "whether or not I have faith." Just sow the Word and the promises that pertain to your particular need instead. Then stand ready for attack, preserving and keeping the Word. Do not act in unbelief by digging up your field every day. By sowing in this way, the Word will produce a faith of substance and certainty. You just know that you know that what God has promised is true.

You will know He is faithful. You know His Word is for you. You know He has spoken to you through His promises. You know He stands by every one of them, because He is a covenant God. You know that He keeps His promises. And you enter the rest of faith, free from anxiety about your circumstances. With the eyes of faith you see what is unseen, and you are "certain of what you do not see." You are convinced of what the Word says, and can therefore approach God free from doubt.

Because you pray in faith you know that you will have what you ask for; you have a certainty and confidence that God has promised to answer your prayers.

There are no short cuts to receiving a miracle. There is no quick and easy method for getting what we need. God is not like that.

But, on the other hand, God is not reluctant and does not want to make life difficult for you. He is willing to help you with everything, and has therefore given you His covenant Word.

That is why it is important that you become rooted and grounded in the Word, so that you know His will and hear His voice more clearly. There is no limit to what God wants to do in and through your life.

Jesus said He would manifest Himself to those who keep His words and follow His commandments (John 14:21, 23). Since we *walk by faith, not by sight* (2 Corinthians 5:7), we need to get into His Word and believe what He says. Then we will *see*.

God stands behind every word He has spoken. Every one of His promises are 'Yes' and 'Amen' in Christ Jesus (2 Corinthians 1:20). His promises are not perhaps and maybe, they are Yes and Amen. He has spoken. He has promised. He has blessed. He has entered into a covenant with us through Christ Jesus, and His Word reveals the blessings He has given us. His final testament has made His utmost will clear. He has said His 'Yes' and is just waiting for you to say your 'Amen'. Then the blessings from His Word can begin to flow in your life.

The power of His Word will begin to work for you. You will have a foundation on which to stand that no one will be able to shake; the revealed of Word of God. You need only say 'Amen' and let His Word be sown within you and it will produce miracles in every area of your life

3

The Faith of the Inner Man

Romans 10:17 says that faith comes by hearing, and hearing by the Word of God. The Word is the means by which God causes faith to arise and grow. It is eternal and it is spirit and life. God's Word is a supernatural power. His Word is the Gospel. Romans 1:16 says that the Gospel *is the power of God to salvation for everyone who believes*. The Greek word for salvation or saved is *sozo*. This word means more than simply being born again. It also means to 'rescue, 'deliver,' 'preserve,' 'heal,' and have "a sound mind." This then is what the word, salvation—*sozo*—means and consequently, what it contains: salvation, rescue, deliverance, preservation, healing, and a sound mind—all of which come through the Gospel; through the Word. God's Word contains the supernatural ability to produce these results in our lives. How does this happen? Through the Word, which is a seed, sown into our hearts and the harvest of everything that grows from it.

Faith of the Heart

Romans 10:10 says,

For with the heart one believes to righteousness, and with the mouth confession is made to salvation.

The word *sozo* or *soteria* is used here, meaning everything just spoken about. In other words, salvation, rescue, deliverance, preservation, healing, and a sound mind come as a result of believing with the heart and confessing with the mouth. Let us take a closer look at what "believing with the heart" actually means.

God has created man in His image. In Genesis 1:26, He says, *Let Us make man in Our image, according to Our likeness.*

God refers to Himself as *Us*. Is this significant? According to the Bible, God is a triune being. He is Father, Son, and Holy Spirit. Throughout the ages people have tried to figure out just *how* this works; but you can never understand the Trinity with your mind. However, the Bible clearly states that it is so. God is three and one at the same time and that each of the three persons in the Godhead is God, yet God is still one. Hallelujah!

So in what way did God create man *according to Our likeness*? Like Himself, of course! Because God is triune He created man triune. God is one so He created man as a whole being. Man is a triune being; He is spirit, soul, and body.

Now may the God of peace Himself sanctify you completely; and may your whole *spirit*, *soul*, and *body* be preserved blameless at the coming of our Lord Jesus Christ (1 Thessalonians 5:23).

God has created us triune and He is interested in keeping us in spirit, soul, and body. He is not just interested in the regeneration of the spirit, but in the preservation of the soul and body as well. Therefore the Gospel, or the Word, contains good news about power for each of these areas. The Word gives new birth (James 1:18), the Word renews our minds (James 1:21), and it heals our bodies (Psalms 107:20).

Man is *one* being with three very different functions.

With his body he contacts and gathers information from the physical world. In his soul, which consists of the will, the mind, and the emotions, he has a consciousness which assembles and processes the information which is gathered from the physical world. And with his spirit, he makes contact with God and can receive information from Him.

The Bible uses a variety of expressions for the spirit of man.

Ephesians 3:16 says, *...that He would grant you...to be strengthened with might through His Spirit in the inner man.*

Ephesians 4:24 says, *...the new man which was created according to God, in righteousness and true holiness.*

1 Peter 3:4 calls it, *...the hidden person of the heart.*

2 Corinthians 5:17 calls it, *...a new creation.*

Ephesians 1:18 says, *I pray also that the eyes of your heart may be enlightened* (NIV).

These are all different names for the same thing; your spirit, your heart, or your inner man. God is a Spirit (John 4:24), and because we are born of the Spirit, we too are spirit (John 3:6).

The moment you were born again, the Spirit of God recreated your spirit and then took up His dwelling there. Your spirit became a new creation in Christ Jesus, and the Spirit of God now bears witness with your spirit that you are a child of God (Romans 8:16).

A *new man* was created within you—that is your spirit, your heart. Your spirit was created to be like God (Ephesians 4:24), and is a partaker of the divine nature through His Spirit. This is the real you. If you were to die right now, your inner man would go on living in eternity.

When we say that your spirit is the real you, we do not mean to say that your soul and your physical body and are not real. They most certainly are. Your body is tangible and real. God created the whole you and is interested in the whole you. That is why He has provided physical healing. But you are more than a body; you have a precious treasure within you which is your true personality—your inner man, your spirit, or your heart.

Some people assert that the spirit and soul are the same thing. But that is not the case. If it were so, 1 Thessalonians 5:23 would not mention spirit, soul, and body individually, and Hebrews 4:12 would not say that the Word of God is sharper than any two-edged sword, piercing even to the division of the soul and the spirit. If dividing between the spirit and soul is a special function of God's Word, there must be some difference between the two which makes it possible to separate them.

So man is spirit, soul, and body.

According to John 3:6 we are spirit beings and the most natural place for a spirit being is "in the spirit." You are far more than just a body or even just a body and soul. You are a spirit being and you have an inner man who, through the Spirit of God, maintains unbroken contact with God Himself; with His glory, power, and wisdom.

It is vitally important that you bear this in mind as we talk about faith. Faith does not come from the body. You cannot believe with your body. Nor does faith come from the soul. You do not believe with your mind, will or emotions.

Faith comes directly from the heart. You can believe only with your spirit. This is why Jesus talks about not doubting in your heart, but only believing (Mark 11:23). That is why Romans 10:10 says that with the heart one believes to righteousness and Ephesians 1:18 (NIV) mentions the eyes of your heart. *Faith is a product of your regenerated spirit.* That is where the Spirit of God dwells. 2 Corinthians 4:13 states that you have received *the spirit of faith.* This Spirit feeds, supports, and helps faith to grow in your spirit or your heart. How? Through the Word which is spirit and life.

34

God Wants Your Inner Man to Grow Strong

The Word of God is a seed full of spirit and life. As it is sown in your heart, the Holy Spirit takes hold of it and causes faith to spring up and produce supernatural results. 1 Peter 2:2 states that the Word is the sincere milk which gives nourishment to your inner man so that he can grow from being a baby to becoming mighty and strong. Paul prays for this to happen in Ephesians 3:16 when he says, *that He would grant you to be **strengthened with might** through His Spirit in the inner man*. God wants your inner man to be strong.

When God created Adam, He wanted him to have dominion over, subdue, conquer, and take care of the creation (Genesis 1:26, 28). Now that God has recreated your inner man to be like Him (Ephesians 4:24), He wants *it* to have dominion, subdue, conquer, and possess. That is why He often tells you to *be strong in the Lord and in the power of His might* (Ephesians 6:10).

Some people have misunderstood this to mean that God loves the strong and despises the weak. How ridiculous! The point is that God wants *His* strength to dwell in you by His Spirit so that your spirit can become strong. God can then have dominion in your life and His power will be present to strengthen, guide, help, and encourage you so that you will become a channel for His power to all those who need it.

Jesus is our perfect example. He walked with God and lived in His Word. By using the Word which had been planted in His spirit and speaking it out of His mouth (Matthew 4:4), He beat back the attacks of the devil. And after He had been tempted and had defeated the devil, He then returned to Galilee in *the power of the Spirit* (Luke 4:14). God's power was flowing through Him and He was strong in spirit. Then what did He do? Matthew 4:23 tells us,

Now Jesus went about all Galilee, teaching in their synagogues, preaching the gospel of the kingdom, and healing all kinds of sickness and all kinds of disease among the people.

Because He was strong in the power of the Lord, He was able to communicate power to those who needed it. This is the Gospel; the power of God unto salvation to everyone who believes.

The Soul—The Place where Two Rivers of Information Meet
God wants your inner man to grow in strength and to be filled with His Word and faith. As we have seen, faith comes from the heart and not from the intellect, will or emotions.

Hebrews 11:1 gives us this definition of faith. It is ...*the proof of things we do not see and the conviction of their reality* (AMP). What does this mean? It means that faith is a conviction about things which my body cannot see, feel, taste, hear, or smell. It is a conviction which goes far beyond my understanding. It is a conviction which goes deep into my spirit, even though I cannot see it, feel it or understand it.

I may not see the answer to my prayer with my physical eyes, but I can see it with my spirit. The eyes of my heart see what God has said in His Word. The Spirit of God paints a picture within me, and with my eyes of faith I see what God has promised. Then I can be convinced that no matter how things look on the outside and regardless of the circumstances, what God has said in His Word will come to pass.

Mental assent is something which closely resembles true faith, but as we have already said, faith is not a product of the soul or the mind. (This does not mean that God is anti-intelligence, just that He is a little bit wiser than you are!)

God has created you as spirit-soul-body. Through the various functions of your body, you are able to receive the information necessary to live in this world. This is important since we shall be in this world until the day we die. It is here that God wants to establish His kingdom through us. When you cross the street, you do not do it "by faith." You look to see whether the light is red or green, and if it is red, it registers with you and you take the necessary precautions to avoid being run over! If you smell smoke in the house you check to see if there is something burning and if so, you save your life by getting out of the house.

Neither do you go outside "in faith" when it is cold; you put on warm clothes so that you will not catch cold or freeze to death!

Your body's physical senses keep you informed about the world around you and provide you with the information vital to life.

Your spirit also supplies you with information, but this time about the spiritual realm and it enables you to live there and maintain a right relationship with your Father and do His will. So you receive information from two different sources and the meeting place for this information is your soul. Your soul is made up of your will, your emotions and your intelligence—or your mind. This is where information is processed and interpreted so that relevant and correct decisions can be made.

And do not be conformed to this world, but be transformed *by the renewing of your mind*, that you may prove what is that good and acceptable and perfect will of God (Romans 12:2).

Fear—The Opposite of Faith

We have all of us—to a greater or lesser degree—been under the influence of the nature of this world. The prince of this world rules, dominates, and indoctrinates the people of this day-to-day world, and given the opportunity, he will do the same to believers too. He will try to fill their minds with as much rubbish as he possibly can and get them to carry out his will. He is always busy trying to influence our minds. Why? Because he wants to rule and have dominion over us.

The weapons he uses most are lies and fear. He tries to give every one of us a picture of who we are, what the world is like, and who God is—a picture which is an utter *distortion* and a *lie*, making it possible for him to steal, kill, and destroy our lives. He wants to take away our hope. He wants to steal our personal initiative and true self-esteem and replace it with discouragement, passivity, condemnation, and inferiority. He wants us either to walk around depressed and full of self-contempt or in the other ditch, full of pride and contempt for others.

Once he has succeeded in painting such a picture in someone's mind and has them believing it, he can manipulate them into doing his works, and so they become an assistant in the expansion of his kingdom.

His most effective weapon is fear. A person who is driven by fear is ready to believe rumours without checking the facts. He is easy to manipulate and does not dare to go against the opinion of the majority. He is afraid of being lonely and abandoned and is prepared to pay whatever it costs to get a pat on the back. A person who is driven by fear lives in constant torment.

Fear is the opposite of faith. Just as faith releases the power of God, fear releases the power of the devil and gives him room to cause havoc in people's lives. Fear is the essence of "the spirit of this world" and is the weapon used by the devil to dominate people (Hebrews 2:14-15). That is why there is so much fear in both the secular and the religious worlds. People are not governed by what the Word of God says, but by what their leaders say. It is a herd mentality, and people hide themselves in the pack. They do not ask, "What does God say?" but rather "What do my neighbours, my leaders or the newspapers say?"

Throughout the ages, fear has been the weapon the devil has been using against the work of God.

People whose minds have not been renewed and aligned with the Word of God are influenced by fear, threats, and lies, and they never dare to verify, never dare to question what they hear. Fear of man rules, rather than the fear of God and many allow themselves to be robbed of God's blessings because they are ruled by fear.

For this reason the Spirit of God is dealing with fear more than anything else today. He does not want fear to rule His children. He wants us to be ruled by *faith* and have our minds renewed, so that by having the correct information we will be able to make the right decisions.

The Spirit of the Lord once said to me, "There's nothing wrong with ninety per cent of believers. They love Me and want to follow Me. It's just that their information is wrong."

Often without being aware of it, we have been programmed according to the world's way of thinking rather than to the Word of God. That is why we are often led by unbelief, doubt, criticism, and fear rather than being led by the Spirit and governed by the Word.

Because of this the Spirit of God is emphasising the Word more than He has ever done before. The same Word which gives rebirth to your spirit is able to heal your body and renew your mind. God wants your mind to be re-programmed with His Word. Some people will, no doubt, cry 'brain-washing!' when they hear this, often without even listening to what is being said. No, it is rather a question of renewing your mind so that the mind of Christ can begin to take over in your mind.

The devil has brain-washed and indoctrinated Christians so thoroughly that the supernatural element, which should be natural for believers, is experienced as something strange and unnatural and fills the unrenewed mind with fear. The devil has been so successful in this that many believers feel more comfortable with their hobbies and activities, reading the evening paper and watching TV, than in spending time in prayer, living in the Word, and seeing the Spirit of God manifest Himself.

No wonder some people react in the flesh when the Word of God confronts them and they discover their lives are miles away from where the Bible says they ought to be! The unrenewed mind jumps up and says, "It can't be that simple! Don't I have to do something myself? It can't simply be a question of just believing! I can't understand this so I'm not going to believe it!"

Listen to the Right Information

If you have the wrong information you are bound to make the wrong decisions, even if you are a devoted Christian.

If you are on the way to Paris and ask for directions, but get information which lands you up in London, you have gone wrong somewhere. The person who gave you directions may have been considerate and well meaning and sincerely trying to help you. The problem is you still ended up with the wrong information. Many of us have received wrong information from well-meaning people who had not been established in the Word of God and had their minds renewed. The question has not to do with whether the person did wrong, but whether the information you received is in line with the Word or not.

Many entrenched traditional thoughts and doctrines sound good, but they fail to hold up in the light of the Word. God wants your mind, your soul to be impregnated with His Word so that you begin to think His thoughts. Then you will be able to make the right decisions and see the power of God released.

For example, suppose God begins to speak to your spirit about something He wants you to do, but what He says seems to be in conflict with the circumstances you see around you. This is exactly what happened to Abraham. God told him that he would have a son. That made absolutely no sense in the natural! What did his body say? "You're too old!" Even his wife Sarah was too old. Besides this, they had never had a child before. What did his mind say? "This is impossible! Abraham, do not make a fool of yourself, forget these absurd and foolish thoughts. You have to face up to reality. You cannot deny what you see! This just will not work!"

How many times have you heard your mind, your reason, your soul speak to you in a similar way? How many times have you given in to your circumstances or agreed with what your mind and senses have said? And how many times have you let go of your 'wild' thought, "sobered up," and let your mind and senses decide for you? What really happened? You let go of the supernatural. Your unrenewed mind, your emotions, and your circumstances talked you out of it, and you missed your miracle.

We have all been there one time or another! And why is this? Because our minds and our understanding took over and began to rule us. Your soul and your circumstances—physical or social—came into agreement, and what God had put in your spirit was in the minority and was voted out. But now instead of being full of fear, your mind gets to be renewed by the Word of God. What happens then? To begin with, as it says in Hebrews 4:12, you will find it much easier to divide between spirit and soul. You will begin to see where the differing influences are coming from.

Secondly, when your inner man begins to speak the Word, your soul gets accustomed to listening to what God has to say. Then, when you find yourself in a situation which requires a decision, you will not just listen to what your circumstances, your mind, and your feelings are saying. You will look at what the *Word* says and you will find your soul saying yes to what is in your spirit.

Your inner man will be in the majority and have the freedom to rule. Life, power, and revelation will come forth and the supernatural will be manifested in the world around you. God will work miracles for you. This is exactly how God intended for you to live;

41

from the inside out. If you live out from the life and faith that are within you, the power of God, available through the Holy Spirit dwelling in you, will flow out to touch and change your surroundings.

This is what happened to Abraham. Romans 4:20-21 says,

He did not waver at the promise of God through unbelief, but was strengthened in faith, giving glory to God, and being *fully convinced* that what He had promised He was also able to perform.

Mental Assent as Opposed to True Faith

As we have seen, faith comes from the heart and not from the mind. When you believe in God, your intellect holds certain facts to be true. You believe, for example, that God is omnipotent, that Jesus rose from the dead on the third day, that the apostles performed miracles in the name of Jesus, and so on. You know these things to be true. This is essential, but knowing them is not enough. To have faith is not merely to agree that a bunch of theological or Biblical statements are true. Faith is much more than that. Faith is trusting in God, expecting every good thing from Him, having fellowship with Him, and willingly obeying what He says.

James 1:22 says, *But be doers of the word, and not hearers only, deceiving yourselves.* In other words, it is possible to hear the Word and yet be deceived, nullifying any possible supernatural results.

How does this happen? By hearing the Word and intellectually agreeing with it, but never grasping it with the heart and acting on it. How does that happen? As the Word comes to me it registers in my soul. "Yes, that sounds right!", I say. So I nod my head in agreement and I might even go so far as to shout, "Hallelujah!" Then I go home and forget all about it, because out there in the real world I follow different rules. Though I hear the Word, I never receive it as though it were meant for me personally.

However, when God speaks, He always speaks to you personally! It applies to *you*, not someone else; it has to do with the *here* and the *now*, not somewhere else or some other time. God has a plan for your life. He wants to help you, He wants to bless you, He wants to use you. When you understand this, your inner man will take hold of it, and eventually you will see a supernatural harvest in your life.

Make Jesus Lord of Your Life

That is why it is so important that you have made Jesus Lord of your life. Tell Him now that He is your Lord. Give every area of your life to Jesus and proclaim Him there as Lord. As your Lord He will have certain things to say about these areas, and because you have made Him Lord, you are in a position to hear from Him and to do what He tells you.

You will be ready to obey His voice as soon as He speaks, whether through His Word or to your inner man. You hear who is speaking and are ready to believe Him. Your mind has found its rightful place and no longer oversteps its authority, but instead submits to your spirit. The supernatural is in control.

Faith of the heart sees beyond the limitations of intellect and circumstance. Faith never *denies* mental or physical reality, as that would be foolish. However, it does not allow circumstances to have the final word. It looks right past the circumstances and into a more real reality.

This reality is Christ (Colossians 2:17) and when I have to choose between what He says and what my intellect or the circumstances say, I choose His Word. Then the supernatural power in His Word is able to change the circumstances. And while this is taking place, the faith of my heart is "certain of what it does not see," my mind is being renewed by the Word, fear is held back, and the rest of faith gives me the *peace of God, which surpasses all understanding* (Philippians 4:7).

4

Whatever You Ask in Prayer, Believing, You Will Receive

Matthew 21:22 says,

And all things, whatever you ask in prayer, believing, you will receive.

This is quite a statement. Jesus puts no limits on what faith is able to receive. When people read a Scripture like this they often hop over it or pretend it is not there or begin to reason it away mentally. "Yes, but *all* things can't really mean *all* things," they say, "It just means some things." We have been so influenced by religious unbelief and ways of thinking which do not expect anything from God, that we unconsciously 're-read' Scriptures like this, putting something else in its place. But "all things" actually means *all* things—*everything*.

Everything always means Everything

In Mark 11:24, Jesus says, ***Whatever*** *things you ask when you pray, believe that you receive them, and you will have them.*

John 15:7 says, *If you abide in Me, and My words abide in you, you will ask* ***what you desire***, *and it shall be done for you.*

John 16:23-24 says, *Whatever you ask the Father in My name He will give you. Until now you have asked nothing in My name. Ask and you will receive, that your joy may be full.*

Contrary to our reasoning, Jesus puts no limit on what can be obtained by praying and walking in faith. In Mark 9:23, He says, *...all things are possible to him who believes.* And when He says all things, He means *all* things. That means *everything!* The words all, everybody, and everything are without limitation. We are often limited by our mind, our experiences, our flesh, other people, and the devil—who, of course, would rather that we did not see a single promise of God fulfilled in our lives.

Because Jesus says, *And all things, whatever you ask in prayer, believing, you will receive* (Matthew 21:22). Then it is an absolutely certain promise that we will receive what we pray for, if we pray in faith.

That is why the devil attacks your faith more than anything else.

We have said that faith is being certain of what we do not see (Hebrews 11:1 NIV); and that faith comes by hearing the Word (Romans 10:17). The more time I spend in the Word, the more I will see of the invisible—the supernatural. And the more I see of it, the more certain I will be about it. The more certain I am, the easier it will be for me to ask for a certain thing. And when I ask for it, according to what Jesus has promised, I will receive it.

Why should it work this way? The Bible says that we should live here by faith and not by opinions (2 Corinthians 5:7). Why is this? To find out, we have to go back to the Fall; and look at how it was before the Fall, and how it was after.

Fellowship With God Builds Faith

Faith is walking with God, having fellowship with Him, and trusting in Him. This is what Adam did prior to the Fall. When we enjoy fellowship with God today, we cannot see Him as Adam

45

could. Nonetheless, God wants us to have the same degree of fellowship with Him, and the same comprehension of Him as Adam had. This will make it so much easier for you to release your faith.

When God created Adam, He created him in the image and likeness of God (Genesis 1:26). Man was created to be like God. Man was not created to be God, but to be *like* Him, fashioned after His likeness. Man received a personality, like God. He received the ability to think, feel, and make decisions just like God. Like God, he was given the ability to talk and carry out various tasks.

God gave him dominion over all creation (Genesis 1:26-28) and put everything under his feet (Psalms 8:6). Adam was made the head of creation in order to rule and reign over it just as God rules and reigns over the entire universe. He was to be subordinate to God and to walk in communion with Him. He was to have fellowship with Him and trust in Him. In other words, Adam was created to have faith in God.

Before he fell into sin, Adam was clothed with the glory of God. Psalm 8:5 says, *You have crowned him with glory and honour*. He was crowned with and covered in glory. God is full of glory, and because he was made in the image of God, Adam too shone with glory.

God gave Adam everything he could ever need because God is a God of abundance. One of His names is El Shaddai, which has been translated as Almighty God (Genesis 17:1), but which really means "the God who is more than enough" or "the God of abundance." God's life is an abundant life. This life pulsated through Adam and the glory of God shone about him. God was with Adam, seeing to it that everything He had was made available to him.

Adam's potential was unlimited. He knew absolutely no limitation! He had need of nothing, he made no mistakes, there was no sin, sickness, or death—none of these existed before the Fall, not even in Adam's subconscious. God was his source of everything, and God is unlimited. Life flowed out from him to everything around him.

God had commanded Adam to be fruitful and abundantly fill the earth, to subdue and have dominion over it (Genesis 1:28). With Adam's help, the whole earth was to be filled with the glory of God. Through Adam, God would manifest and multiply His life, His glory, and His honour throughout the whole universe; and every element of creation would give praise, honour, and glory to God forever.

God Created Everything Good, Pleasant, and in Abundance
After God created Adam, He planted a garden for him and put him in it to tend and keep it (Genesis 2:15).

We said before that Adam knew no poverty or deficiency in his own life or in his God. God is a good and loving God of abundance, and Adam was acquainted with His personality and knew His character. So when God prepared a place for Adam, He provided something consistent with His very own personality. What did He do? He created a garden and named it Eden. Eden is Hebrew for "richness, abundance, and delight." This is the sort of place where God wanted man to dwell. It was his home prior to the Fall.

Genesis 2:9 says, *And out of the ground the Lord God made every tree grow that is pleasant to the sight and good for food. The tree of life was also in the midst of the garden, and the tree of the knowledge of good and evil.* God caused beautiful trees bearing delicious fruits to grow in the garden. Have you ever wondered why you find yourself attracted to beautiful things or why you enjoy things that taste good? Because they were created for your enjoyment!

Adam had all that. Up until the time of the Fall, God was the centre of his life and his source of satisfaction in everything. So then what happened? Through the Fall, man fell short of the glory of God (Romans 3:23).

When Adam sinned, fear came into his life. The serpent had sown seeds of doubt into Eve regarding God's Word (Genesis 3:1), and when doubt in God's Word took root in them, she and Adam acted on it and sinned. As a result, the glory of God departed from him and Adam realised he was naked. For the first time in his life he became aware that he had needs. Suddenly, a need arose and he was no longer able to draw from God's glory and abundance in order to meet it.

Faith is communion with God, walking with Him and having fellowship with Him. The more you have fellowship with God, the more you get to know Him. And the more you get to know Him, the more you appreciate Him. The more you appreciate Him, the more you trust Him. And the more you trust Him, the more you know that He always keeps His promises and does what He says He will do. This is what faith is all about.

Sin-Consciousness and Fear Keep Us Away From God

Communion with God had now been broken and something totally different from faith came in: fear. In Genesis 3:10, Adam says, *I heard Your voice in the garden, and I was afraid because I was naked; and I hid myself.* Fear had already begun to dominate man—and it has done so ever since. Fear is the opposite of faith. It causes man to hide from God rather than come to Him with confidence. Fear comes from a consciousness of sin and the feeling that one is not right with God, as well as from the inability to supply one's own needs and shortcomings.

Fear is a powerful force which brings ruin and destruction in people's lives. Hebrews 2:14-15 tells us that Jesus came so that *through death He might destroy him who had the power of death, that is,* *the devil, and release those who **through fear of death** were all their life-time subject to bondage.*

Fear is the weapon the devil uses to enslave people. Because it drives man away from God, it prevents him from having fellowship with God and getting to know Him. If man does not get to know God, he will readily believe lies about Him. The devil paints a picture of God which is entirely different from the one given by the Bible.

The devil's picture is of a schizophrenic, incomprehensible, and remote God who is without loving care for people and their needs or problems. He drums this picture into people's minds to keep them from enjoying their share of God's blessings. When someone whose mind is filled with this picture of God reads, *all things, whatever you ask in prayer, believing, you will receive* (Matthew 21:22), he finds it unreal, strange and sometimes even frightening. But why is this? Because he is so far removed from seeing the true picture of God, and knowing the fellowship with God that Adam had before the Fall.

Jesus Christ, however, came as the last Adam in order to restore our communion with God. God can once more be to us the One He has always been: El Shaddai, the God of abundance, the God who meets you and satisfies you in every area of your life.

God is Satisfied With the Sacrifice of Jesus

Before Adam fell into sin, there was not a single area in his life wherein God did not totally meet his needs and satisfy him with Himself. God had more than enough to offer him in every area of his life. But when Adam fell, everything was affected. Even today, the Fall has affected every single area in the life of mankind.

It has damaged our spirit, our soul, and our body; our relationship with God, with other people, and with nature; and our social and financial needs. Everything has been affected by it.

Prior to the Fall, faith ruled in these areas. But after the Fall, fear came in through sin and began to rule. Man became afraid of God—but do confuse this fear with having the fear of the Lord. To fear the Lord is having respect for God and at the same time knowing Him as a Father. It is not a panicky terror of a God who constantly needs to be appeased with sacrifices lest He punish you.

This wrong concept of the fear of God lies at the root of every one of the many varieties of religion and religious behaviour, which try to appease God—buy Him—with sacrifices to win His favour and stop His attacking you.

Paul talks about this in 1 Corinthians 10:20 when he says, *But I say that the things which the Gentiles sacrifice they sacrifice to demons and not to God...*

The devil found an entrance through the fear which gripped man after the Fall. He distorted man's spiritual hunger for God and darkened his understanding (Ephesians 4:18; Romans 1:21) so that fear motivated him when he sought God. The result was that man began to listen to demonic lies about the character of God and the way to gain peace with Him.

This need for peace, together with a fear of punishment, gave rise to man's many efforts to do good deeds and make sacrifices in an attempt to reach God. Religious behaviour in general is equivalent to the fig leaves Adam and Eve used in their own attempt to cover their nakedness after their glory had gone.

In himself, man can never do what is required to get back to God. This is why God sent Jesus: to be a free gift of God's own righteousness to those who would receive. When we receive by faith what God has done for us, we no longer need to be afraid of Him or try to satisfy or appease Him. He is already satisfied with what Jesus has done for us on the Cross. When we accept this we are given His righteousness and we regain our right standing before God—the standing that Adam lost.

Before the Fall, Adam was able to have fellowship with God with no sense of guilt, shame or inferiority, and God was accessible to him in every area of life. As we have seen, after the Fall, this was no longer so, but now, through Jesus Christ, God has opened a way for us so that everyone who *believes* in Jesus has received his right standing before God again. Once again God is available to us in every area of our lives, just as He once was for Adam.

Our lacking knowledge of this has kept us from seeing just what kind of relationship we have with God through Christ Jesus. The same fear that entered through sin has even influenced our Christian life and changed it from a supernatural life—one in which God has supernatural fellowship with us and works in and through us—to a religious life dominated by fear, condemnation, and natural limitations. God did not redeem us from the curse of the law (Galatians 3:13) so we could walk around in condemnation and inferiority. He has cleansed us from an evil conscience so that we may come boldly to the throne of grace to obtain mercy and find grace to help in time of need (Hebrews 4:16; 10:19-23).

Through the blood of Jesus, God has cleansed us from an evil conscience so we can come boldly before His face and enjoy the same level of fellowship with Him that Adam had, able to receive all the help we need in every area of our lives. Fear, condemnation, and ignorance of God's character and His Word will keep you away from His presence and glory. But there is no longer any condemnation to those who are in Christ Jesus (Romans 8:1).

The Glory of God Dwells Within You

God has delivered us from condemnation, cleansed us from an evil conscience. Now, we are free to come to Him at any time and receive help in every area of life. The difference between us and Adam is that we walk not by sight, but by faith (2 Corinthians 5:7).

Adam was clothed with a visible, outward glory and he could see God with his physical eyes.

You have God's glory on the inside of you, and you see God in your spirit. According to Ephesians 4:24, your new man—your spirit—is created to be like God. Because the Holy Spirit dwells in your inner man the glory of God is present within you. It is there that he meets with you, and you are able to see Him with the eyes of your inner man (Ephesians 1:18).

The reason you must walk by faith in this world is because the devil still exists and rules over those who are under his dominion. With faith, however, you are able to overcome the world (1 John 5:4-5) and see the manifest glory of God (John 11:40).

How were the disciples able to see the glory of God? They said, *we beheld His glory, the glory as of the Only Begotten of the Father...* (John 1:14). How had they seen the glory of Jesus? As it flowed from Him in the form of supernatural miracles which abundantly met people's needs.

In John 2:11, we read about His first miracle, turning water into wine at a wedding in the town of Cana: *This beginning of signs Jesus did in Cana of Galilee, and manifested His glory; and His disciples believed in Him.* The glory of God was manifested when Jesus did miracles.

When Lazarus became ill and later died, Jesus said, *This sickness is not unto death, but for the glory of God, that the son of God may be glorified through it* (John 11:4). How did the sickness of Lazarus glorify Jesus? Was it by Lazarus faithfully carrying his sickness without having his needs met? No, it was when Jesus raised him from the dead that the glory of God was revealed!

The glory and the life that Adam knew, he lost in the Fall (Romans 3:23). So God sent Jesus to reveal this glory and return it to man. God's glory was within, upon, and around Jesus. He walked in this world as a light which shines in the darkness *and the darkness did not comprehend it* (John 1:5).

The glory of God is manifested in this world through miracles which meet people's needs. Jesus forgave sins, healed the sick, cast out evil spirits, raised the fallen, restored lost self-worth, broke the bonds of condemnation and inferiority, and gave people's lives meaning and purpose.

Through the new birth, the glory of God has come to dwell within you. The same Spirit of glory lives in you and wants to do the same things in your life. God wants to make you a channel for His glory out to the people around you. But because we live in a world which is dominated by an enemy called the devil, and because we cannot physically see the glory of God in the way that Adam was able to see it, God has had to provide a means for us to participate in His glory. This means is called faith.

Did I not say to you that if you would believe you would see the glory of God? (John 11:40).

God Has Given Us Everything With Jesus

As a believer the glory of God dwells in you through the Holy Spirit. The new man within you is created in the image of God and you are righteous in Christ. Because of the blood of Jesus you are therefore entitled to fellowship with God as your Father. You can come boldly before Him without feeling guilty, ashamed or inferior, and you can partake of and enjoy all the good things He has for you and has done for you. He has done for you as much as He did for Adam. What God was to Adam, He is also to you. God is no respecter of persons. Just as He placed His omnipotence, His abundance, His wisdom, His power, and His glory at Adam's disposal, He has placed all these things at your disposal through Jesus.

God is omnipotent, which means that He *is able* to do anything. The question is whether or not He *wants* to. But God is also love! And because God is love, it means He is willing to put everything He has at your disposal. The Gospel is the good news that God loves us. The Gospel reveals *the things which God has prepared for those who love Him* (1 Corinthians 2:9). What has God prepared for us? Romans 8:32 says,

He who did not spare His own Son, but delivered Him up for us all, how shall He not with Him also freely give us all things?

He has actually *blessed us with every spiritual blessing in the heavenly places in Christ* (Ephesians 1:3). Everything He has and everything He is, He has placed at our disposal. If He has already given us the most precious thing He had—Jesus—should not He be willing to give us the things that are far less precious; such as healing, guidance, financial blessing, and so on? He said that He would give us *all* things with Jesus.

This is the picture of God we need to get into our spirits: that God is exactly who the Bible says He is, and not what religious traditions, misconceptions or feelings of condemnation tell us. He is the God who met Adam's every need.

He is the God who revealed His glory in and through Jesus Christ. He is El Shaddai, the God who is more than enough. He is the One who meets every one of your needs in *every* area of your life. Why? Because He loves you! Because Jesus says He is like that. That is why Jesus says, *And all things, whatever you ask in prayer, believing, you will receive* (Matthew 21:22).

When I see just how good God really is, it is easy for me to believe that He is willing to meet my every need. I am set free from religious misconceptions that prevent my receiving from Him. Because God put Adam in the garden and gave him pleasant and beautiful things, met his every need, and gave him dominion over this world, I can see that God wants to do the same for me. Through Christ Jesus He is my God of abundance as well.

The devil will always try to steal from us in as many areas as possible. He is a thief who comes only to steal, kill, and destroy. He is also a liar from the beginning. With his lies, he tries to make us believe that there are areas in our lives which God has no interest in. He has convinced many that God does not do miracles, that God does not heal people. And if by chance He might be willing to heal someone, it certainly would not be you. So, there is no point in praying for healing, after all one never knows what God's will is.

The same applies to your finances. "God would never be interested in anything so ugly. Would God bless anyone financially? It's completely out of the question! It would only make you proud or greedy."

No one who truly loves the Lord, wants to become greedy or proud. So the devil easily scares us away from something he says is dangerous, and we never take the time to find out for ourselves what the Bible says. Obviously, God does not want you to be greedy or proud, but He has a way of letting His blessings flow over you, and at the same time keeping you in godliness and holiness so that your first priority is to seek Him and follow Him in everything.

God wants His life to surround you and bring you miracles in every area of your life, including your health and finances. He is interested in the whole of your life, not just a part of it. When you see God's character, what He has, and what He has made available for you in Christ, you will find it so much easier to believe that He actually does want to give you *all things, whatever you ask in prayer, believing...*

5

The Gospel is the Power of God to Salvation for Everyone Who Believes

Romans 1:16-17 says that *the Gospel of Christ...is the power of God to salvation for everyone who believes... For in it the righteousness of God is revealed from faith to faith; as it is written, "The just shall live by faith."*

We have heard this Scripture many times, but we have rarely thought about what it really means. The word Gospel means "good news." God has come to you with news of something good. The Gospel is the Word of God, so the Word is good news for you and contains the power of God to salvation.

The word, salvation means more than simply being born again. In Greek, it means "salvation, deliverance, preservation from the evil of this age, healing, and sanity of mind." So the Gospel contains the power of God unto salvation in every area of your life. Not only does it include the regeneration of your spirit; it also includes preservation and peace of mind, healing for your body, and protection and deliverance in times of pressure and difficult circumstances.

God is interested in the *entirety* of your life—not just a part of it.

God's Promises Make You a Partaker in His Divine Nature

His divine power has given to us *all* things that pertain to life and godliness, through the knowledge of Him who called us by glory and virtue, by which have been given to us exceedingly great and precious promises, that through these you may be partakers of the divine nature, having escaped the corruption that is in the world through lust (2 Peter 1:3-4).

God is telling us a lot of things here! He says He has given us all things that pertain to life, or in other words, everything we need in order to live. It is deposited for us in heaven, and we can partake of it in this life through the knowledge of Him and His great and precious promises. These promises give us a share of the divine nature.

God's power is in the Word, in the promises, and in the Gospel. And when His promises are in you, by your receiving them and considering them precious and great, when you hear them and act upon them, the power of God will be released to work in you and enable you to escape the corruption in the world. The Gospel is good news which communicates God's power to you and gives you everything you need for life and godliness. It gives you the ability to overcome the world, to escape its corruption and the attacks of the enemy, and to live a life of victory. The Gospel, God's Word, becomes the power of God to salvation in every area of your life.

This is very good news! There is no area of your life where God does not have good news for you! No matter how stuck you are, how miserable your past has been, how many failures you may have had so far, or how many disappointments you have experienced, God has good news for you. This Good News is that Jesus Christ has died and paid the price for your sins. He became a sin offering on your behalf and conquered and disarmed the devil. He has risen again as a champion and is seated at the right hand of the Father, high above every principality and power in the spiritual realm and far above every problem and attack. And today He is alive and is forever interceding for us.

This is the Good News: that the name of Jesus is above every name and every other name must submit to His name. We, the Church, have been given authority to use His name.

This is the Good News: after man had fallen in sin and had come under the control of corruption and the curse, Jesus took our sin and its consequences upon Himself in *every* area of life. He took our *full* punishment and became our substitute. *This* is the good news, and something we need to see and understand. It is important that we see what the Cross means to us, so we can receive what it offers us.

The Gospel of Jesus is the power of God to salvation for everyone who believes. The Gospel is the Good News about why Jesus came to earth. 1 John 3:8 says, ***For this purpose the Son of God was manifested, that He might destroy the works of the devil.*** Hallelujah! That is *why* Jesus came: to destroy the works of the devil—the thief who had been stealing, killing, and destroying people's lives. Jesus came to put an end to this and give people abundant life instead (John 10:10).

The Gospel—The Power of God
to Salvation in Every Area of Life

This is the Gospel: Jesus paid the price for our sins and conquered the devil *in order to give us something better*: abundant life, God's kind of life. He came to bring salvation—rescue, deliverance, healing, and a sound mind wheresoever the devil may have stolen, killed or destroyed.

The Gospel applies to our life as a whole, not just to part of it. Some people might say, "Yes, but being born again is much more important than anything else." Of course, the new birth is certainly the most important thing. Nothing is more important than a person getting saved and escaping eternal death, but why *divide up* the Gospel? If God has provided a full salvation which covers every area of life, then we do not need to pick and choose, nor have we any right to do so.

Jesus paid an extremely high price for your and my salvation. What He went through is indescribable; His suffering was immense. For that very reason He wants to see the fruit of His suffering. He wants to see us using the things He purchased for us. Isaiah 53:11 (AMP) says, *He shall see the fruit of the travail of His soul, and be satisfied.*

The more we receive of what Jesus has paid for, the more fruit He will see, and the greater satisfaction and joy He will have.

God's Gifts are Given to be Used

Imagine a father who decides to give his son a motorbike. It costs so much that he has to work overtime to get the money. Finally, after a lot of hard work, he is able to buy the new bike, brings it home, and gives it to his son. When the boy sees it, he says 'thanks,' puts it in the garage, and never uses it. Instead, he criticises the model, complains that it does not work right, and continues to ride his old, worn out moped which is always breaking down.

Do you think this will bring joy to his father? No, it grieves him. In this same way, we grieve the Holy Spirit when we do not properly appreciate what Jesus has done for us and show our gratitude by receiving and making use of it. The more we receive of what was accomplished for us on the Cross, the more joy we will bring to our Father in heaven.

What exactly did Jesus do for us? What does the Good News entail? You will only be able to accept and receive what you understand. If you only know that the Gospel contains the regeneration of your spirit, then this is all you will be able to receive. The Gospel will only become the power of God to salvation for you in that area. But when you discover that the Gospel pertains to your entire life, it will suddenly become the power of God in every area.

The Scriptures say that the Gospel is the power of God to salvation for everyone who believes. If, through ignorance or unwillingness on your part, you do not believe that the Gospel is good news for your family life, your future or your health, then God's power cannot operate in these areas, and you will not see supernatural results. The Word has not been sown there, so there cannot be a harvest. Victory is absent and corruption reigns instead. 1 John 5:4 (NIV) says,

For everyone born of God overcomes the world. This is the victory that has overcome the world, even our faith.

We have said that faith comes through the Word of God. When your faith is being fed through the power of the Word, it will have the ability to overcome the world and its corruption, opposition, and attacks.

Ephesians 6:16 says, *above all, taking the **shield of faith** with which you will be able to quench **all** the fiery darts of the wicked one.* Through the Word, faith becomes a shield which will quench *every* fiery dart in your life, wherever and whenever they may appear. Faith in itself has the supernatural ability to overcome the world. Hallelujah!

The Good News is for Today

Faith is believing the Gospel of Jesus Christ and what He has done for us. When we understand that what He has done covers everything, the Gospel will become the power of God for salvation in every area of our lives. Naturally, the devil has tried to steal from us in as many areas as possible in an attempt to stop us from being free.

One of his methods is to place limitations on the Gospel, because if you think the Gospel does not apply to a certain area of your life, you have no right to expect anything from God in that area. The devil will tell you that there are no promises which cover your particular area of need. And if that is the case, you have nothing on which to stand before God and cannot expect a miracle from Him.

It is true that we cannot go beyond the promises of God; we can only pray according to His Word. But glory to God, who *has given us all things that pertain to life and godliness* (2 Peter 1:3), and *who has blessed us with every spiritual blessing in the heavenly places in Christ* (Ephesians 1:3).

Every area *is* covered! The next lie the devil tries is the one which goes, "That was only while Jesus was here on earth" or "That's only for when we get to heaven." He always wants to move the Good News away from the present moment. He does not want you to have anything right now, but constantly tries to keep it away from you, either by pushing it into the past or far ahead into the future.

But, *now is the day of salvation.* Salvation is available *here* and *now* and is *for everyone*, and that means *you*. Everything the Gospel contains is also for you, because God is no respecter of persons. He has made it available to everyone, *everyone who believes* (Romans 1:16), *for the same Lord over all is rich to all who call upon Him* (Romans 10:12), *and whoever believes on Him will not be put to shame* (Romans 10:11).

Jesus Died That We Might Live

What then does the Gospel entail? The Gospel is all about Jesus—who He is, what He has done, and what He is doing today. We have already said that He came to destroy the works of the devil. He also came as our replacement, as a substitute for us, to take our place. It is very important we understand that. He took our place on the Cross so we would *not* have to take that place of shame, punishment, and condemnation, but that we might take *His* place instead. He was "the holy sacrifice," exchanging His place in glory for our condemnation so we could share in His glory. The Cross is a place of substitution and exchange.

What did He carry on the Cross?

He took our sin *so that* we could have His righteousness (2 Corinthians 5:21).

Our chastisement was upon Him *so that* we could have peace (Isaiah 53:5).

He took our diseases *so that* by His stripes we could be healed (Isaiah 53:4-5).

He died *so that* we might live. He was despised, abandoned, and rejected *so that* we could be accepted and loved, and as children of God have communion with Him. He became poor *so that* through His poverty we might become rich (2 Corinthians 8:9). He was made a curse for us *so that* the blessings of Abraham could come to us (Galatians 3:13-14). He set aside His place in glory *so that* we might have a part in it, and so that we could sit together with Him in heavenly places (Ephesians 2:6).

This is what the Gospel includes. Jesus paid the price for our sin and bore its consequences. He broke the power of sin and the devil and has brought us into a new kingdom. Colossians 1:13 says, *He has delivered us from the power of darkness and translated us into the kingdom of the Son of His love*. He has made us partakers of *every spiritual blessing in the heavenly places* (Ephesians 1:3) in every area of our lives.

There's no Sin or Sickness in Heaven—Jesus' Victory Applies Today

The Gospel covers every area of your life. Man has fallen in every area of life, but through Jesus there is salvation for all of it. He took all your sin and sickness upon Himself *so that* you might enjoy His abundant life. This is the good news!

Then someone says, "That'll only happen in heaven." No, it is for today! Heaven will be wonderful, but victory is already a reality for us here and now! The shield of faith quenches *all* the fiery darts of Satan right *here*! You will not have to fight against him in heaven because he is not going to be there!

Your faith overcomes this world and its influence. The world is *here* and *now*! There is nothing of the world in heaven! Some people say, "Forgiveness is for today, but healing is only for heaven." That is wrong. The price Jesus paid on the Cross was the same for both your sins and your sicknesses. He has never separated these two things, as in unbelief, we have done.

Isaiah 53:4-5 reveals that Jesus took both our sins and our sicknesses. Psalm 103:3 says, *Who forgives all your iniquities, who heals all your diseases*. Clearly, the Cross dealt with both of these things. The Gospel has good news of victory over both sin *and* sickness.

While Jesus was on earth He not only forgave sinners, He also healed the sick (Mark 2:9-11). He forgave the sin of the man with palsy at the same time that He healed him. At this point, someone usually says, "Yes, but Jesus only healed back then." No! If healing was only for those days, then forgiveness was only for those days! If healing is only going to take place in heaven, then forgiveness will only take place in heaven. If healing is just for a select few, then forgiveness is also just for a few. But that is not the case!

Everything Jesus accomplished on the Cross has been made available to *everyone*. These are blood-bought covenant rights for *all* who believe in the Gospel of Christ. The Gospel is the power of God to salvation for everyone who believes, in *every* area of life. If the Word does not say anything else about your situation, then you can assume that there is help and victory for you here and now.

Of course, if the Word makes any restrictions, you have to go along with them. You cannot pray that you will not have to die, for example, since physical death is the last enemy which has still to be placed under Jesus' feet. We will all die one day, unless Jesus comes to take us home as the last living generation, but Jesus has broken the sting of death, its power and its threat. For the believer, death is nothing more than a doorway into eternity (1 Corinthians 15:54-57). Until it comes, however, God wants you to live your entire life in victory and know the power of God through the Gospel in this present life.

Humility Is Taking God's Promises Seriously

God does not want us to separate what He has joined together in the Gospel. He wants us to appreciate and receive everything Jesus accomplished *for* us on the Cross. Nothing will bring Him more joy than to see us receive and appreciate what He has given us.

It is not prideful to speak loudly about God's promises; it is, in fact, humility. Humility is believing that what God says is true. It is letting your own personal thoughts and speculations yield to His Word.

But pride always explains away the Word and puts question marks where God has put exclamation points, and questions and criticises when God offers and gives. Pride sometimes disguises itself in a kind of religious 'humility' which says, "This is just too great or unbelievable" or "Oh, yes, but not for poor, little old me. As long as I'm saved, I'm content."

That is not humility. Humility is finding out what God says and then acting accordingly. If what He offers you includes every area of your life, you are humble when you boldly expect victory in every area of your life. This brings great joy to Jesus, who paid a high price to give you victory.

Some people say, "But that sounds so egocentric and self-centred. Isn't the Gospel meant to be about God?" Yes, of course it is about God. Of course God is central. He is the One we worship and honour. Jesus is the One we exalt and praise. But the Gospel is actually the good news that *God so loved the world that He gave His only begotten Son, that* [notice the purpose] *whoever believes in Him should not perish* [notice this concerns the life and needs of the individual] *but have everlasting life* (John 3:16).

Then others will say, "But we don't believe in God just to receive things, do we? It can't be that selfish." Yes, that is exactly what you do. You believe in Jesus to *receive* eternal life. When you confess Him as Lord you receive forgiveness, righteousness, and new life. God sent Jesus so you could *get* something, *be* something, and be able to *do* something.

False humility says, "I'm nothing, need nothing, and expect nothing." But the believer says, "I was nothing, but through Jesus I now have something wonderful. I am somebody and I can do something. I have received everlasting life, I am a child of God, and I am here to serve and glorify Him."

God sent Jesus to give you something, and when you receive it, you in turn, have something to pass on to others. Peter said in Acts 3:6,

Silver and gold I do not have, but what I do have I give you: In the name of Jesus Christ of Nazareth, rise up and walk.

What did this man need? Healing power from God. And what did Peter have? The power of the Holy Spirit. He had first received it for himself, and when he had received it he was able to give it to others. (You cannot give what you do not have.)

The Gospel is the power of God in every area of your life. When your cup is full, it will run over and from your belly will flow rivers of living water. You will be able to give to others from what God has given you. You will preach what you have seen, heard, and experienced, about how Jesus meets your needs, forgives your sins, gives you victory, answers your prayers, and guides you through life. This is what you have to give to others. God wants you to live in the fullness of the Gospel so others can also be blessed.

6

The Righteous
Shall Live by Faith

I am not ashamed of the Gospel, because it is the power of God for the salvation of everyone who believes: first for the Jew, then for the Gentile. For in the Gospel a righteousness from God is revealed, a righteousness that is by faith from first to last, just as it is written: "The righteous will live by faith" (Romans 1:16-17 NIV).

We have said that the Gospel is the power of God to salvation for everyone who believes. The above Scripture tells us that the righteousness of God is revealed in the Gospel and that the righteous shall live by faith. This is something of great importance.

For many people, however, the word 'righteousness' seems strange and abstract. It sounds so theoretical that just hearing it is enough to make them lose interest. But when the Holy Spirit brings the reality of righteousness to life, it becomes extremely interesting and releases immense power in one's life.

The Bible tells us that the righteous shall live by faith. Only when you understand the meaning of righteousness can you truly begin to live by faith and see victory in the areas of your life that now know only defeat.

Righteousness—A Tremendous Force in Your Life

Righteousness is not just some theoretical doctrine—it is a tremendous power in your life.

Romans 5:21 says, *as sin reigned* [meaning ruled and had dominion] *in death, even so grace might reign* [in this life] *through righteousness to eternal life through Jesus Christ our Lord.*

This will become powerful for you when you grasp and understand it with your spirit. Righteousness is a power which will rule, reign, and take dominion in your life so that God's eternal, abundant life has the place of victory and control.

We have already seen that the Gospel is good news for us in every area of our lives. The devil knows this, so he tries to make us feel unworthy to receive what God has given us. Receiving it, you receive it in faith. Hebrews 11:6 says,

But without faith it is impossible to please Him, for he who comes to God must believe that He is, and that He is a rewarder of those who diligently seek Him.

If God says in His Word that we are to believe that He will reward us when we seek Him, it is not difficult to conclude that the devil is going to attack us in this area. In Hebrews 4:16, we are exhorted to *come boldly to the throne of grace, that we may obtain mercy and find grace to help in time of need.*

The Gospel has something to offer us! God wants to *give* you something. He wants to reward you and give you help in time of need! We are therefore exhorted to *come boldly* to Him with the expectation that He will reward those who diligently seek Him.

The devil hates such boldness and tries as hard as he can to destroy it. He knows that if he can take it away from you, you will not go to God to receive help and you will not be able to live in victory over him. That is why the devil does not want you to understand righteousness. This understanding will give you the boldness you need to go before God at any time and receive all that the Gospel has for you. Because of this, the devil persistently beats a wrong sin-consciousness into believers, causing them to constantly feel condemned and rejected, and to flee from God rather than boldly going to Him with their problems.

We mentioned earlier how fear entered man through the Fall and how the devil has been using it to entangle and rule him (Hebrews 2:14-15). Through the Fall, mankind became aware of sin and lack and condemnation. He has lived in a constant awareness of his need, his shortcomings, and his deficiency ever since.

The Entrance of Sin and Death

Man who was created in the image of God, clothed in glory, who he walked in dominion over creation as a king in submission to the King of kings, lost all this and became a slave to sin and the devil. Sin began to reign and take dominion over him (Romans 5:21). Death and the fear of death began to rule him (Romans 5:17). The devil's way of destroying man was to cause him to despise and look down on himself and to be ruled by the anguish and condemnation brought on by his true sinfulness.

Man had taken on part of the devil's nature, he was spiritually dead in himself, and walked according to the spirit working in him (Ephesians 2:1-2). He was bound by sin, a slave to his own lusts, and incapable of setting himself free. His conscience witnessed against him and he knew that he was not right with God. Condemnation was his master.

Today, though they reject the existence of God, many people go to great lengths to appear good, self-fulfilled, and successful. They will do virtually anything to remove their guilt, liberate themselves, live out their emotions, and attain self-fulfilment.

This however, is all in vain—the equivalent of trying to empty the Atlantic Ocean with a spoon. There is no way to deliver oneself from feelings of guilt; the underlying, *real* guilt cannot be taken away. Self-fulfilment cannot be attained so long as the fallen, sinful nature remains. Therapeutic efforts are therefore useless; like trying to pick yourself up by your own bootstraps. The dissatisfaction, guilt, inferiority, and feelings of insufficiency and condemnation remain.

Standing in a Garage Does Not Make You a Car

Positive thinking and even ambitious goals will not help. New Year's resolutions soon fail, and the disappointment and dissatisfaction increase. Standing in a garage and calling yourself a Volvo does not make you a car! You have to be *changed into* one! That is why Jesus said, *You must be born again* (John 3:7).

When you are born again the old man, which is your sin nature, dies within you and through the Holy Spirit the nature of God comes into you. You become a new creature in Christ with a totally new nature. You are set free from sin (Romans 6:18, 22) and the law (Romans 7:5-6), which constantly accused you of not doing enough or being good enough. The old spirit of bondage which continually kept you in fear disappears, and you receive the Spirit of adoption instead (Romans 8:15).

The New Birth Makes You a Righteous New Creation

What does all this mean? You must understand that two things happened when you received Jesus Christ. *First of all*, you were declared righteous because you received the righteousness of Jesus. He is perfectly righteous and has never done anything unrighteous. When you see Him doing things in the Gospels, you see how a righteous man should act.

Jesus was the first truly righteous man since Adam to walk on earth in perfect communion with His Father. He did the works of His Father and the glory of God was revealed through Him. He did not walk around in condemnation, shame, insecurity or confusion. He knew who He was, where He was going, and what He had to do. His circumstances did not rule over Him, He ruled over them. The righteousness within Him reigned in His life wherever He went. He laid down this righteousness when He became *your* sin and died for you, so that you could have *His* righteousness (2 Corinthians 5:21).

When you proclaimed Jesus as Lord, His righteousness became your righteousness. Because of His death, His sacrifice for your sins, and His resurrection and victory, God was able to declare you righteous and you have received His righteousness. This means that just like Jesus, you can come boldly before God without feeling guilt, shame, insufficiency or inferiority. All this is due to the righteousness of Jesus which became yours when you confessed Him as your Lord. You have been clothed in His righteousness.

The second thing that happened when you were born again was the exchange of your old heart for a new one. You received a new nature and a new spirit. A new man who had never before existed was born within you; a man who partakes of the very nature of God (2 Peter 1:4). Through the Holy Spirit dwelling within this new man, God's unlimited resources are available to him. Just as you were completely dead in your sins, you have become completely righteous in Jesus.

Your nature was totally sinful, but in Him you have received a new, divine nature. It is through this Jesus' nature, and not your own; it is through God's righteousness and His Word, and not your own ability or strength that you now have an unlimited potential for victory. Ephesians 6:10 exhorts us to become strong in the Lord, but it is in the power of *His* might. The power of His might

70

has been infused into your spirit by the Holy Spirit and has been made available through the righteousness of Christ.

This puts a totally new perspective on your life and causes the devil to change his tactics immediately. Before you received Jesus, he tried to keep you away from Him by saying, "You don't need Jesus, you're getting along just fine without Him." He complimented you on your abilities, your talents, your looks, on your intellectual capacity, your strength of will, and so on. This was all just to keep you from seeing your need for Jesus. But all the while, your conscience was defiled and you felt condemned and dissatisfied.

Now, however, you have been born again. The debt is paid; you have peace with God and your nature is new. There is no longer any condemnation.

Never Listen to Condemnation

Romans 8:1-2 says, *There is therefore now **no** condemnation to those who are in Christ Jesus, who do not walk according to the flesh, but according to the Spirit. For the law of the Spirit of life in Christ Jesus has made me free from the law of sin and death.* No longer do you have to run away from God in fear and shame like Adam. You can come before God free from guilt and inferiority. The way to the throne of grace is always open to you. God is with you and for you. All of His promises are available to you.

When the devil sees this, he completely changes his strategy. Rather than making you feel successful in your own strength, as he used to do, he tries to make you feel that you have nothing, can do nothing, understand nothing, and will never be able to do anything for God. He has deceived many generations of God's wonderful children with these lies. He beats on your flesh to get you looking at your weaknesses and to make you think that you will never be able to improve.

The Bible tells us that there is a side of our lives which is carnal. Your flesh will be with you as long as you live in this world, but you do not need to live according to its demands (Romans 8:4). Because you have been born again, you are no longer a debtor to the flesh (Romans 8:12). Through the Spirit you are told to put its deeds to death (Romans 8:13).

We should not sow to the flesh, the Bible tells us, because if we do we will reap death. Instead, we should sow to the Spirit, and reap life (Galatians 6:8). If we walk in the Spirit, we will *certainly not* fulfil the lusts of the flesh (Galatians 5:16).

What does this mean? It means that even though your flesh will be with you for the rest of your life and will always resist and be at enmity with God (Romans 8:7), victory is available to you through the Holy Spirit working with your born-again spirit. You no longer need to live according to the flesh and experience defeat. You can live in the Spirit and walk in victory as a result.

In spite of what many people preach and teach, the Bible tells you that you *can* walk in the Spirit, that you *can* live in victory, and that *sin shall not have dominion over you* (Romans 6:14). There is victory for every situation! How? By faith!

When you are born again, the devil tries everything to take away your victory. He gets you to think that you can never live in victory and he points to the many failures and miserable circumstances of your life, as proof of how worthless you really are.

Here is where you have to live by faith. When you see yourself as righteous, you will be able to do this. You are not a poor sinner any more. You are not even a sinner who has been saved by grace. You were a sinner, you had a fleshly nature (Romans 5:8, 7:7), you were saved by grace and have now been made righteous with the righteousness of God Himself.

God Looks at You as Though You Were Jesus

When God looks at you, it is as if He were looking at Jesus, or as He looked upon Adam prior to the Fall. He does not see your sins—He sees your righteousness in Christ. Does this mean you are perfect and completely free from sin? No, it just means your sins do not count any more because of the blood of Jesus. You will always sin and make mistakes in this life. That is why you have been given access to the blood of Jesus, because it is with His blood that God can cleanse you from *all* unrighteousness when you confess your sins (1 John 1:9).

Hebrews 10:17 says, *Their sins and lawless deeds I will **remember no more**.*

God forgives, blots out, and totally forgets your sins. When He looks at you, He does not see all that you have done wrong. When you have confessed your sin, He only sees the blood and the righteousness of Jesus which has become yours. You are made righteous in His eyes. If you are in Christ, God looks upon you as He looked upon Adam, and you can enjoy fellowship with Him, love Him, and work with Him without any feelings of condemnation or fear.

This does not mean you should exalt yourself above God or become filled with pride. God is God, not you, but you can take your rightful place in creation as one who has been made in His image. Your position is beneath God, but above creation so that you can take dominion and work together with Him.

This is what the devil is afraid of. He is terrified of a generation of Christians who know who they are in Christ. He knows that when we understand who we are, what we have access to, and what we can do, his influence over us and the rest of the world is broken. It is then that we will be free to win this world for the Lord.

Satan attacks righteousness to stop you from boldly taking hold of what belongs to you through Jesus' redemptive work on Calvary. He lies to you by telling you that you are not worthy. But you are!

You were unworthy, but even then God demonstrated His love toward you. *While you were still a sinner,* Christ died for you (Romans 5:8). Even though you did not deserve it, God sent you the best that He had. He paid a high price for you while you were still a sinner. How much more will He give to you now that you are righteous?

You are a Joint-Heir with Christ

Jesus has made you worthy. In Christ you have received the title of son, heir, priest, and king. You are no longer unworthy. You are a son in the household of God with the rights of an heir and the authority of a subordinate king.

The Holy Spirit wants to develop your consciousness of righteousness, so that it is much greater than the wrong sin consciousness you once had. There is both a right and a wrong sin consciousness.

A right consciousness of sin comes by the conviction of the Holy Spirit (John 16:8-11). When He does this, He speaks clearly and understandably and without room for escape. He names the time, the place, and the victim of the crime and, above all, offers you a solution—the Cross, the blood, and His forgiveness. *He convicts rather than condemns in order to set you free.*

But when the devil comes, he accuses and condemns. He offers no hope and says you are beyond help. If he cannot nail you with anything in particular, he will cast a cloud of self-reproach, guilt, and self-contempt over you without offering a way of escape.

If you resist what comes from the devil by standing steadfast in faith, he will flee from you (James 4:7; 1 Peter 5:9). He is a prosecutor who no longer has the right to bring up your case. You have already been judged, and the verdict was "Not Guilty". Someone else has taken your punishment: Jesus was found guilty, you have been spared. Because you have accepted what He has done for you, there is no longer any condemnation or guilty sentence.

You do not need to pay attention when the devil comes to accuse you with the law. Why? Because you are dead to sin and the law on all accounts (Romans 7:1-6, 6:2, 7), and he cannot continue accusing someone who is dead. Colossians 2:14 says that Jesus has *wiped out the handwriting of requirements that was against us, which was contrary to us. And He has taken it out of the way, having nailed it to the Cross.*

Dead People Need Not Reply

If you consider yourself dead to sin (Romans 6:11), you can remain neutral toward the devil's accusations when they come. You are not even obliged to reply. You are no longer subject to the devil's laws or even within his jurisdiction. You belong to another kingdom now; one in which Jesus is your advocate and intercessor, and His task is to make constant intercession for the saints. When you confess your sins, you allow Him to plead your case. If you do not confess what you have done wrong, however, He has nothing to work with, and you will have to solve your own problems and stand in your own defence—and that does not work very well! But, if you confess your sins, Jesus can plead your case not before the devil, but before the Father. He will plead your *innocence*. God will listen. The verdict of "Not Guilty" will stand and you can go free.

Who shall bring a charge against God's elect? It is God who justifies. Who is he who condemns? It is Christ who died, and *furthermore*, is also risen, who is even at the right hand of God, who *also makes intercession for us* (Romans 8:33-34).

If God is for you, who can be against you? You have a wonderful position as a child of God. When you walk in faith and believe what

Jesus has done for you, and what He is doing for you this very day at the right hand of the Father, there will no longer be any room for condemnation. Your days of torment will be over.

You no longer need to go around listening to the devil's lies and accusations. You no longer need to go around oppressed, confused, and full of self-condemnation and self-reproach. You see what Jesus has accomplished for you on the Cross—and that is all you need. You understand that you are no longer a sinner, but that you have been made righteous in Christ. You are a child of God and God's heir. You can stand up and take your rightful place. You are not ashamed of the blessings of God, but can enjoy them and pass them on to others.

Let Righteousness Reign—It Will Bring You Victory

In the same way that sin used to rule and reign in your life and fear used to haunt you, now grace through righteousness prevails *even more* (Romans 5:20-21). You are no longer a slave, but a free son of God, in right relationship with Him, and with His life flowing from you to greatly bless others.

God wants our consciousness of righteousness to far exceed the consciousness of sin we used to know. The reign of sin was one of total dominion in our lives, controlling both our thoughts and our actions. But now we are righteous. Where sin has had a great influence, God's grace will abound all the more, and righteousness will dominate us to a greater extent than sin has ever done.

When the devil tries to get you to concentrate your attention on your weaknesses and failures, Colossians 3:2 tells you to, *Set your mind on things above, not on things on the earth*. What does this mean? It means that God wants us to fix our thoughts on what is in heaven: the treasures and resources we have available to us, the present-day ministry of Jesus as He makes intercession for us, and the righteousness we have been given. That is what God wants us to fix our thoughts on!

We should be much more conscious of our righteousness than of our sin!

When faith becomes the substance of things we do not see, it will look beyond every circumstance and attack and see the position we have in Christ. And this position is that we are more than conquerors, that we are seated in the heavenlies with Christ, to Whom every principality and power in the spirit world is subject. Faith sees the reality of this righteousness even when you do not feel righteous or the circumstances are up against you. This is how grace through righteousness reigns in life. God's life can flow out of us. Self-condemnation or insecurity are no longer a hindrance to us. We know, when we hear from God and also when we do not. We do not doubt and we are no longer confused. There is a clarity to our life in the Spirit.

Hebrews 5:13-14 tells us that the word of righteousness, through practice, helps us train our senses so we can discern both good and evil. When we are firmly established in the righteousness of God, we are not so easily confused or accused. We have the ability to expose the devil's lies and schemes (2 Corintians 2:11) and can recognise what is good, as well as what is evil.

As a result of the devil's condemnation and accusation, there has been a tremendous amount of confusion in this area and many Christians have actually mixed up good and evil.

God is good and gives only good things (James 1:17). The devil is evil and *does not come except to steal, and to kill, and to destroy* (John 10:10). Unfortunately, however, we have resisted the gifts of God by thinking they do not belong to us, or that we do not deserve them. At the same time we have received what comes from the devil, being led to believe that it comes from God to serve "some higher purpose which we cannot comprehend." We have believed that "there must be some sort of purpose behind it all." But now those days of confusion are gone forever!

Righteousness Makes You a Bold Mediator of God's Life

Hosea 4:6 declares that God's people are destroyed for lack of knowledge. Today, however, the Spirit of revelation is flowing through the Word of God and is sweeping aside traditional thoughts and doctrines which have no basis in the Scripture. The light of the Gospel and its true significance is shining forth.

We can see that we have been made righteous through Christ and that our position *in* Him and *with* Him is at the right hand of the Father.

We understand that the familiar prayer, "Thy will be done on earth, as it is in heaven," means that God desires for all that He has in heaven to come to us and to be put to work here on earth.

We can see that we do not need to beg for grace when we have already received it and can stand in it as righteous sons and heirs in the household of God (Romans 5:2).

We hear God telling us the same thing the father told his oldest son in Luke 15:31, *Son* [for now we are truly sons!] *you are always with me,* [through the blood of Jesus we have constant access to the Father], *and all that I have is yours* [in Jesus the Father has placed everything at our disposal]. We have a rich inheritance which is more than enough to meet every one of our needs.

Philippians 4:19 says, *my God shall supply **all** your need according to His riches in glory.* God is good and loves us dearly. He has wonderfully restored communion with us and tells us to come boldly to His throne of grace (Hebrews 4:16).

The awareness of our position in righteousness will produce great boldness within us to act on God's every promise and communicate His life and power wherever there are needs. In this way we will bear much fruit and our Father will be glorified (John 15:8).

7

Faith Speaks

Romans 10:10 says, *For with the heart one believes to righteousness, and with the mouth confession is made to salvation.* Up to this point, we have talked about the faith which comes from the heart; what it is and how it is obtained. We have also looked at righteousness and salvation, and seen that the word 'salvation' implies more than simply being born again. This word also means rescue, deliverance, preservation, healing, and soundness of mind. All of this is made available to us through the faith of the heart, faith that is *certain of what we do not see* (Hebrews 11:1 NIV).

This certainty comes as a result of the Word of God and the confession of our mouth. We have often skipped over or failed to understand just how important our words are in seeing the things that God has for us become a reality in our lives.

Several years ago, I wondered why there were so many wonderful, devoted Christians who loved the Lord and yet never saw the power of God released in their lives. Then one day the Lord said, "The power is escaping from their mouths." He showed me a picture of a pressure cooker with an open valve from which the pressure was escaping only to be wasted and disappear. The Lord used this illustration as a key to help me understand the immense importance of our words.

The Universe is Held Together by the Word of God

The spoken word is often held in low esteem. We say things like, "it's just talk" or "all talk and no action." Through newspapers and television, broken election promises, and our own abuse of the spoken word, we have little or no understanding of just how important words really are.

The Bible, however, has a totally different view of the power of our words. In Matthew 12:36, Jesus says,

But I say to you that for *every idle word* men may speak, *they will give account* of it in the Day of Judgement..

Jesus regards *every word* we say as important—so important, in fact, that one day we will give an account for every idle word we have spoken. Why is this? The answer lies in the nature of God, in the way He has constructed the universe and made it function, and in the nature of man.

The whole universe functions and is held together by words. Hebrews 1:3 speaks of Jesus as *upholding all things by the word of His power.* His words hold the entire system together.

We have already said that God is a God of faith. His heart is full of faith and from His divine faith the Holy Spirit put faith into our hearts when we were born again. The Word of God is the means by which the Holy Spirit causes our faith to grow and become active.

As God planned the universe, He had an inner picture of what He wanted. He had a plan, a purpose, and a vision in His heart. He believed it. He was convinced of it, although the plan had not yet been realised. Neither man, nor the earth, nor the universe itself was yet in existence. Nothing was visible except what His inward eyes were able to see. His faith saw that which was to come.

Then one day everything was physically manifested. How? God spoke it out! Genesis 1:3 says, *Then God said, "Let there be light";*

and there was light. God spoke and the world came into existence. He said 'be' and it was. As these words went out of God's mouth, His power was released and what was in His heart in the form of a picture and a conviction became a manifested, physical reality.

How? By the power which flowed out from His Word.

So shall My word be that goes forth from My mouth; It shall not return to Me void, But it shall accomplish what I please, And it shall prosper in the thing for which I sent it (Isaiah 55:11).

The words that God sent forth from His mouth, His spoken Word, were containers of His power. So that it was released and created what He desired.

Psalm 33:6 says, *By the word of the* LORD *the heavens were made, And all the host of them by the breath of His mouth.* Verse 9 continues, *For He spoke, and it was done; He commanded, and it stood fast.*

Man was Created to Rule

Then God said, "Let us make man in our image, in our likeness, and let them rule over the fish of the sea and the birds of the air, over the livestock, over all the earth, and over all the creatures that move along the ground" (Genesis 1:26).

Man should be like God, think like God, act like God, and speak like God.

God is a King. His Word is commands which go out. They are commands which change the state of things. When God created man, He put him in a position of dominion over creation, saying fill the earth and subdue it (Genesis 1:28). Psalm 8:6 says, *You made him ruler* [which means co-regent, subordinate king under God] *over the works of your hands; you put everything under his feet* (NIV).

Man was appointed to the high and lofty position of leadership over the earth. Psalm 115:16 says,

The heaven, even the heavens, are the LORD's; But *the earth He has given to the children of men.*

He gave man authority and dominion over the earth. But how were we to carry out this responsibility? In the same way God does! We have been created in His image and after His likeness.

How does God rule? As a King! His Word goes out, and His commandments bring things to pass. Man was meant to rule in exactly the same way. He was created to work in cooperation with God, and his words were meant to create, establish, and bring things to pass.

What was born in mankind's heart and had been painted as a picture within him as a result of his close fellowship with God, had to be spoken out and then the creative power of God would be released through him. We can see this exemplified in Adam's naming of all the animals which God brought before him (Genesis 2:19).

So what went wrong? The devil came and sowed doubt concerning the Word of God (Genesis 3:1, *Has God indeed said...?*), causing man to fall into sin and die spiritually.

In order to see this in context, we need to understand that Adam had been given authority here on earth. He was placed here to rule in word and in deed. The devil wanted to steal this authority, and in order to do so, he sowed doubt in the reliability of God's Word and caused man to believe and act upon *his* words instead. This gave the devil the right to steal, kill, and destroy people's lives—something he has been doing right up to this very day!

How? By influencing our words. He gets us to believe his lies and speak in line with his intentions, so our words give him the permission he needs to perform his work in and through us. Why does he have to do it this way? Because you and I were created to rule here on earth. Both God and Satan desire to establish their kingdoms here and our faith and the words we speak are the channels through which they are able to do so.

Words full of faith release the power of God. Words filled with doubt, criticism, unbelief, hatred, etc., release the devil's power and give him free reign to cause havoc. Why? Because we were created to be kings, a position we have regained through the new birth. 1 Peter 2:9 calls us a *royal priesthood*. Revelation 1:6 says that Jesus *has made us kings and priests to His God and Father.*

The definition of a kingdom is: "the domain over which the king has jurisdiction; a sphere of power or influence." The decrees of the Swedish government, for example, are valid in Sweden, but not in Norway. They have no jurisdiction there.

In the same way, you have been given responsibility for your life and family. The words you speak out have authority in these areas, and can either be spoken in the service of God to release His power, or in the service of the devil, releasing his power. What you say is not unimportant. What you speak out about and over others, for example, your children will affect them far more than you realise.

Words are creative and will influence and build things within the spirits of men. Because the devil knows this he wants to steal our words; thus allowing him to stop the power of God and carry out his work in people's lives.

Your Words are Creative: Talk Like God

One person who understood the power and authority of words was the centurion with the sick servant in Matthew 8:8-10. He said to Jesus,

Only speak a word, and my servant will be healed. For I also am a man under authority, having soldiers under me. And I **say** to this one, 'Go,' and he goes; and to another, 'Come,' and he comes; and to my servant, 'Do this,' and he does it. When Jesus heard it, He marvelled, and said to those

83

who followed, "Assuredly, I say to you, I have not found such great faith, not even in Israel!"

Why did Jesus marvel and praise the centurion's faith? Because he understood the significance of words. The centurion knew that what Jesus spoke would release the power of God because of Jesus' position of Lordship. *He believed in the power of faith-filled words.*

Jesus walked on earth, holding the same position Adam had had prior to the Fall. With His words He healed the sick, rebuked storms, cursed the fig tree, raised the dead, and fed thousands of people. He did this to show us the true nature of God. In everything He said and did, Jesus was the perfect expression of God's will here on earth. At the same time He was the Son of Man, a name He often called Himself, who came to demonstrate the true essence and ability of a man. He is man in reality.

When you were born again, you were placed "in Christ". We are His body here on earth and we are called to follow Him and to do His works (John 14:12-13). We are God's children and that is why the Word says, *therefore be imitators of God, as dear children* (Ephesians 5:1).

We are members of God's family and like children in any family, we are bound to sound like our Father. In every family the children's behaviour patterns and means of expressing themselves reflect their parents. The same is true in the family of God.

The word 'imitator' in Ephesians 5:1 is the Greek word *mimetai* which means to 'mimic.' Just as natural children imitate their earthly parents, so are we to mimic or imitate God. What does this mean? It just means, be like Him, so that His character is our character, so that we talk and act as He does. This has been something totally foreign to us because we have not understood our position in Christ. But now that we have become the righteous children of God, our Father wants us to speak like He speaks. We do this by speaking His Word; by saying exactly what He says.

The Good Confession

The Bible has a lot to say about the confession of our mouths and its importance. Romans 10:10, in fact, tells us that it is by our confession that we are saved.

The Greek word for 'confession' is *homologeo* which means, "to say the same as". When you confess something, you are saying the same thing someone else says. Unfortunately, this is something which has often been understood only in negative terms. 1 John 1:9 talks about the confession of sin, but this is only one type of confession in the New Testament. When you confess your sin, you are simply agreeing with God about what you have done wrong. His forgiving power is released when you say what He says.

The devil has abused this principle by getting people to constantly talk about how sinful they are and how unworthy they are. He has drawn, in their spirit, a wrong picture of their true nature. Your words *create*, both in yourself and in others. But confession means more than just the confession of sin.

Hebrews 10:23 tells us to *hold fast the confession of our hope.*

1 Timothy 6:12 talks about the *good confession.*

Hebrews 3:1 calls Jesus *the Apostle and High Priest of our confession.*

Confession is saying what God says about you in every area of your life. It is agreeing with everything He says concerning us. It is speaking out what He says concerning Himself: who He is, what He has, and what He wills. It is speaking out what Jesus has accomplished for us. It is *saying* who we are in Christ, what we have access to, and what we can do through Him. It is naming our position above our enemy; that he has been conquered and is able to do very little.

You might say, "Do I really have to say it? Isn't it enough just to believe or think it?" 2 Corinthians 4:13 says,

But since we have the same spirit of faith, according to what is written, "I believed and therefore I spoke,' we also believe and therefore speak.

If you believe in something and are convinced about it, what you believe will come out of you. You will speak about it, and it is vital that you do. Out of the abundance of your heart your mouth will speak, be it positive or negative.

Some people say, "I don't believe in rattling off a bunch of Scriptures. It sounds to me like hocus pocus or mantras repeated over and over." These people have not even begun to understand what the Bible says about words. Instead, they are usually ensnared by their own words which have released death in their lives.

Proverbs 18:21 says, *Death and life are in the power of the tongue.* What does that mean? It means the tongue has in its power the ability to bring about life or death. Words full of slander, suspicion, envy, hatred, criticism, control, manipulation, and lies create a tremendous seed bed for the works of the devil. Where words of unbelief, doubt and criticism prevail, the works of the devil are released and he is given permission to carry them out.

James 3:16 says, *For where envy and self-seeking exist, there is confusion and every evil thing will be there.*

Before we became Christians, or even when we were lukewarm, carnal Christians, we let our flesh determine our speech. We spoke what *we* thought and what *we* felt, and nothing at all of what God said in His Word. People are often ashamed to speak what the Word says if it does not seem to be in line with what they see at the moment.

For years the devil has indoctrinated us with the information we have received through our minds. The morning and evening papers, as well as religious publications have communicated negative and incorrect information which has moulded our minds in a negative way. Very often, our speech is negative and filled with fear and unbelief. We say things like: "This will never work", "I don't know how to do anything", "Things are just getting worse", "I'll never make it in time", "I'm afraid I can't", "I don't see any solution" or "Nothing ever seems to work for me, no matter how hard I try."

Our Words are Taken Seriously in the
Spirit World—They are Royal Commands

We may not take the things we say really seriously, but in the spirit world our words are given utmost importance. We may joke and not really mean what we say, but if we were to realise that our words are royal decrees, we would not say things like: "See you tomorrow, if I don't get run over by a train, Ha! Ha!"

We talk to cars and tell them off if they do not start. We yell at the threshold when we stumble over it, scold buses, rain clouds, and so on, and no one thinks anything about it. We prophesy in the negative that our things will fall apart, that we will miss the bus, and so forth. To most people this is completely normal. Why? Because we have heard and received information that has been negative and deceitful. We have believed, spoken, and acted upon the lies and fears with which the devil or "the spirit of this world" has indoctrinated us.

When God comes to help us change, the flesh may react by saying, "What a mechanical method, just rattling off Scriptures like that." This is the carnal mind turning against the Word of God. You should be turning against the flesh instead! Put God's Word in your mouth and speak out what He says concerning your situation no matter how it feels.

In the beginning it may seem dry, mechanical, and strange, but what was it like when you were learning to walk? You did not sit there and say, "I don't feel anything, so this can't really be working. I've already tried walking three whole steps without seeing any results!" No, keep at it, take in the Word of God in every way you can. Confess daily what God says about your situation—after all, for years you may have been agreeing with the devil.

Confession works in two ways: 1) To faith and 2) From faith.

Confessing "to faith" means that you begin to speak God's promises from the Word over a particular situation in your life. You will have to work hard at this, since the devil will attack the Word and do all that he can to make you feel uninspired, mechanical, or legalistic. Just keep going! Read the Word, meditate on it, and speak it out. It will be built into your heart and suddenly it will become a confession "of faith," from *your* faith, from *your* heart. You will discover that where you used to react with fear, panic, disappointment, and bitterness, now the Living Word will come speeding out of your spirit, moved along by the power of the Holy Spirit, like a huge locomotive under full steam.

That Word that goes out of your mouth, "tidies up" in the spiritual realm. It sweeps aside all resistance and releases the power of God. The Word is a two-edged sword (Hebrews 4:12), but it is not a weapon to be used in fighting against other Christians. It is a weapon in the *spirit world.* How does it work? Revelation 1:16 says of Jesus that, *out of His mouth went a sharp two-edged sword.* In the same way, the Word which goes out of *your mouth* is a two-edged sword against the enemy.

Psalm 8:2 says, *Out of the **mouth** of babes and nursing infants You have **ordained strength** [the Swedish translation says power], *Because of Your enemies, That You may silence the enemy and the avenger.*

God has put power in our mouths. What kind of power? It is the power of His Word, which when it becomes a weapon on our tongues, beats down the enemy. God's Word has the same power in your mouth that it had in the mouth of Jesus. Jesus told the devil, *"Away with you, Satan! **For it is written**..."* (Matthew 4:10). If Jesus needed to use the Word as a weapon to stop Satan, do you not think you will need to do the same? It is not our power; it is the power of the Word in our mouths which stops the enemy.

No wonder the devil tries so hard to prevent the believer from spending time in God's Word and then speaking it. But we speak the Word; we do not speak the circumstances, we speak what God says *about* the circumstances. "Oh," some people say, "But we can't deny reality." No, we cannot, and there is no reason why we should. Reality, however, is much more than what we are presently able to see with our physical eyes.

We need to distinguish between faith facts and physical facts. If you have a pain in your leg, then you have a pain in your leg. Your leg is not well. If someone asks you if you are in pain, and with a strained smile you reply, "Oh no, I feel just fine," then you are telling a lie. This is wrong and will inevitably stop the power of God.

There is no reason for you to deny that your leg hurts, that would be foolish. What you should do instead is speak what the Word says about your leg, rather than merely agreeing with what your leg is telling you all the time. Everything in this world, including pain, is subject to change. Pain is not permanent. *For the things which are seen*, 2 Corinthians 4:18 says, *are temporary, but the things which are not seen are eternal.*

Speak the Word to the Mountains

This means that in spite of how they may look, each and every circumstance in this world can be changed. Circumstances are only temporal. The Word of God, however, is eternal and has a higher value. The invisible existed before the visible; therefore what is seen must submit to the unseen. Faith is a conviction about the things I do not see (Hebrews 11:1).

The Word is eternal and cannot pass away or change (Matthew 24:35). When you have received it sown into your heart, faith will grow and you will begin to see in the realm of the invisible. With your inner eyes you will see the change that you need, the miracle that you need. What God has shown you in His Word will become a conviction in your heart.

Of course, you feel the pain in your leg, so do not deny it. Its voice speaks loud and clear, but at the same time you hear another voice and see something else—something which God has shown you in His Word. You see that by His stripes you were healed (1 Peter 2:24). You see your healing, grasp it with your faith, and speak it out with your mouth. "Yes, my leg hurts, but by the stripes of Jesus I have received healing and the power of God is working that healing in me."

This is exactly what Jesus talks about in Mark 11:23-24 when He says, *Whoever **says*** [not thinks] ***to*** [not about or concerning or speaking with others about] *this mountain*, *"Be removed and be cast into the sea," and does not doubt in his heart, but **believes** that those things he **says** will come to pass, he **will** have whatever he **says**.*

Jesus is telling us that we can have what we say. "But surely," someone may say, "we can't have everything we say, can we?" In the next verse Jesus says, ***whatever** things you ask when you pray, believe that you receive them, and you **will** have them.* In other words: If faith, certainty, and conviction from the Word is in my heart concerning my particular mountain, circumstance or problem, I will not doubt. Then I will not speak as though the mountain were something final as if it will always be there. In my heart, through faith, I see what God says. His Word reveals His will to me and I know, I am convinced that He does not want that mountain to be there. He is for me and not against me. So what do I do? I release His power through words full of faith. I speak *to* the mountain, a royal edict is issued and a command is sent forth which tells the mountain to move.

To whom? To the mountain! Speak directly to your circumstances, not just to somebody else about them. Do not pity yourself to get sympathy, just speak to the mountain. Because I have now seen God's will, something within me will refuse to accept the circumstances and demand a change. But, some people say, "How can we refuse to accept something that's right there?" Because you are able to see beyond it! You speak to the mountain and command it to go! "Yes, but what if it's still there, anyway?"

Jesus only asks us to do what He Himself practised. A few verses earlier, in Mark 11, He had cursed a fig tree. He spoke *to* the tree (Mark 11:14), but not until the next day did the disciples *see* that the leaves had fallen off and the tree had withered

(Mark 11:20-21). The instant Jesus spoke, the Word went out of His mouth and what He said took place in the spirit world. The root was cursed, but it took time for a visible manifestation to appear. Jesus explained what had happened by using the illustration of the mountain which was cast into the sea (vv 23-24).

When you speak to the mountain and command it to be cast into the sea, the Word of God goes out of your mouth and it will not return to you void, even though you do not immediately see visible results. Remember what Jesus said in verse 23, *but believes that those things he says **will come to pass**, he will have whatever he says*. You must hold a conviction that it will be so and that it will come to pass at some point in the future.

Verse 24 reveals something that is important to understand since faith always concerns the present. Jesus says, *believe that you **have** received it, and it **will** be yours* (NIV). In other words, when I pray, when I command the mountain to go, when I confess what the Word of God has to say about the situation, *at that point*, even before I see any visible results, *then* I believe and receive it as fact. I see it accomplished and complete with the eyes of my faith. I see the answer before I have it, and when someone asks about it, I speak the result and not the problem, because I *know* that the solution is on its way. Jesus said, *it **shall** be yours* (v 24).

This does not mean that I deny the mountain's existence, but I refuse to see the temporal as though it were final, because I know what God has said about it. Abraham saw his son long before Isaac was born. Romans 4:18-21 tells us how he behaved. He saw that his own body was as good as dead but he did not let it act as his final source of information. When there was no hope naturally speaking, he still hoped and believed. *He did not waver at the promise of God through unbelief, but was strengthened in faith, giving glory to God, and being fully convinced that what He had promised He was also able to perform* (v 21).

Every hero of faith in the Old Testament had to go through this process, and you and I will have to do the same. And that is wonderful, because it is how we learn to trust God. It is about seeing what God has to say about the situation—despite the circumstances—holding onto it, believing it, confessing it, and seeing His Word fulfilled in our lives.

Hebrews 10:23 says, *Let us hold fast the confession of our hope without wavering, for He who promised is faithful.*

God has spoken. What He says is true. I hold on to the promises of His Word. I say what He says. I agree with Him and say the same things He says without letting my circumstances move me. Why? Because I have close fellowship with Him and know that He is faithful, that His Word can be trusted, and that He is able to perform what He has promised. When I say what God says, I give Him permission and room to work. His power is released and my circumstances change. The temporal must submit to the eternal. The natural must submit to the supernatural.

When the Word of God goes out of your mouth, extraordinary things start to happen. One of these things is the strengthening of your own faith as you hear it spoken. Another is that the Word divides between soul and spirit in your life (Hebrews 4:12), enabling you to see God's will more clearly. The Word also creates as it goes forth. It is a seed which produces a harvest. And finally, it is a mighty weapon which breaks down strongholds and stops the enemy in his tracks.

God has truly put a tremendous amount of power in your mouth (Psalms 8:2). Both life and death are in the power of the tongue (Proverbs 18:21). Words are containers. When they are filled with the Word of God, they are filled with all that His Word contains, namely spirit and life, and God's power is released.

8

The Prayer of Faith

In Matthew 21:22 Jesus says, *And all things, whatever you ask in prayer, believing, you will receive*. This is a tremendous promise that the mind finds hard to grasp and accept. Our minds, in fact, usually raise objections and attempt to tone down or explain away what Jesus has said. The mind that has not been renewed by the Word of God will immediately react with doubt and unbelief to a bold statement of this kind—even from Jesus. Romans 8:6 says, *For to be carnally minded is death, but to be spiritually minded is life and peace*. The carnal mind, containing thoughts and imaginations which have not been brought into obedience to Christ (2 Corinthians 10:5), finds it hard to take the promises of God literally. It always looks for an exception or reservation to avoid having to believe and accept the Word as personal and relevant for today. This was the problem with the children of Israel.

Mix Your Faith With the Promises

God had promised to be their Covenant God. He was their Shepherd, their Provider and their Healer. He was their Righteousness and their Victory Banner, their Peace and the Omnipresent One who was always their God Nearby. Everything He was, He had placed at their disposal through His covenant. Yet, in spite of all this, Hebrews 4:2 tells us, *For indeed the Gospel* [with all that it entailed] *was preached* *to us as well as to them; but the word which they heard **did not profit them, not being mixed with faith** in those who heard it.*

Like us, they also heard the Word, but when they heard the Word and the promises that God offered them, they did not become a reality in their lives. Their prayers were not answered. Why? Because the promises of God had not been mixed *with faith*.

God's promises are like the flour in a batch of dough. But if you do not blend in the yeast, it will never become bread. You can have however much flour, as many promises as you like, but not until the yeast, faith, is added, can the process begin which produces bread.

Faith is the ingredient God has given you. It grows through His Word. When you add faith to the promises, to God's invitations, and take them up as truths, as yours, real for you here and now, then the process which produces a miracle in your life can begin.

All things, Jesus says [not just some things or a few things], *All things, **whatever** you ask in prayer, believing, you will receive* (Matthew 21:22; John 15:7, 16:24; Mark 11:22, 24, to name just a few). When God says something, He means it—especially when it is obvious He has said it more than once. He has put no limits on the prayers you can get answers to. Why? Because God Himself is unlimited; and in His love for you, He willingly puts all His ability at your disposal.

God is also a Covenant God, and through the blood of the New Covenant you have been given blood-bought rights. He has provided for every area of your life and has left nothing out. There is no limitation with God.

But meanwhile Jesus has put a condition on *how* the things of God will be placed at our disposal: this condition is called faith. Jesus Himself said this! It was not just some preacher or faith-teacher, but Jesus Himself! If Jesus has said it, it is in our best interest to submit to His Word. We are not doing ourselves any favours trying to explain it away or getting upset at the word 'faith,' or trying to avoid it, or denying the validity of the promises for everyone today. God has a much better way!

Jesus does not say, *all things are possible to him who believes* (Mark 9:23) to oppress people, but rather to lift them up. When Jesus says, *O, faithless and perverse generation* in Matthew 17:17 or, in verse 20, *if you have faith as a mustard seed, you will say to this mountain, "Move from here to there," and it will move; and nothing will be impossible for you*, He is not trying to reprove people because they cannot believe. His true purpose is to challenge them to put their faith in God. When the Word of God challenges you to believe, it does so to stir up a longing within you to see your heavenly Father do the impossible.

Faith is Not a Demand—It is a Help

Faith teaching is from the Holy Spirit. Its purpose is to activate your faith so you can receive the promises in your heart, and let the process of producing a miracle begin. For this reason the devil wants to make the teaching of faith appear as though it places great demands on you. He wants you to say, "This is too much for me," and so you run away from everything. But that does not solve any problems.

If Jesus says that he who believes will get his prayers answered, then He has certainly provided a way which enables you *to* believe. He helps you activate your faith so you can receive what He is longing to give you. He is *for* you—not against you! Faith is not complicated. When you know God and understand His character, you will realise that *everything* He says is true. Your faith will then become *the evidence of things not seen* (Hebrews 11:1), and because you **know whom you have believed**, your walk of faith with Him becomes a rest (2 Timothy 1:12).

Faith becomes a completely natural part of your life. We are actually created for the supernatural, and the supernatural should be natural for us. That is where God does miracles. Miracles are natural for us. We are created for them. God loves to do them. They are not merely divine interruptions in an otherwise dull and colourless life. Miracles are the norm, and because *the just shall live by faith*, our whole life is to be one of faith—and its resulting supernatural miracles.

Faith becomes as normal to you as using your legs to walk. You do not consciously think about having to lift your foot ten centimetres, do you? No, you just do it! It is a natural part of your life. And that is the way that faith works when you have seen who God is.

Walking, however, did not feel natural when you first learned how! You stumbled many times and there were numerous opportunities to give up. But an infant does not stay on the floor when he falls and say, "This doesn't work, so I think I'll lay here the rest of my life. I'm going to make others carry me and do my walking for me." Neither do we hold special classes for babies to tell them that learning to walk is not really necessary. We do not excuse them by saying, "God loves you anyway." We do not hold courses where we try to lessen the sense of compulsion that they have to walk.

No, there is something within every child that makes him get up again and again until he is able to walk. And those who are watching the child rejoice, offer encouragement, and take part in every little step he takes. And it is like that in our spiritual life, as well.

Every Believer Has Received the Spirit of Faith

There is something within every believer called the Spirit of faith (2 Corinthians 4:13), which encourages, draws alongside, strengthens, and helps the believer to believe. The Spirit, though, must have certain things to work with; these being the Word, its promises, and your will. When the Word is sown in your heart and your will connects with God's promises to the point that you begin to desire what God desires, you will discover what Romans 8:26 means when it says, *the Spirit also helps in our weaknesses*.

This word 'helps' in Greek means "to take hold against together with." The Spirit of God takes hold together with you, to work through you and for you against the problems around you. The Spirit helps you hold on to the Word which has been sown in your heart, so that, contrary to your circumstances, you believe what God has said, just like Abraham did (Romans 4:18-21).

This sort of lifestyle should be normal for you. It enables you to see what is in the Spirit rather than just seeing the natural or physical dimension and being limited by it. Believing can become as natural as walking. And you will be able to walk long distances, happy that you missed out on the course that tried to teach you how to avoid walking!

Your faith is like that; it is like a motor in car that runs without your thinking about it. It is not a heavy demand that makes you ask, "Do I *have* to believe?" Instead, it carries you as long as your engine has fuel, that is, as long as you remain in fellowship with Jesus and the Word of God.

If any of you lacks wisdom, let him ask of God, who gives to all liberally and without reproach, and it will be given to him. But let him ask in faith, with no doubting, for he who doubts is like a wave of the sea driven and tossed by the wind. For let not that man suppose that he will receive anything from the Lord; he is a double-minded man, unstable in all his ways (James 1:5-8).

What are we being told here? God has a reason for speaking these Scriptures.

Verse 5 says that if you lack anything, in this case referring to wisdom (although it could mean anything that the Word of God covers), God has it, and it *shall* be given it to you. This is a powerful promise for seeing your prayers answered! There is a condition, though, attached to this promise.

Verse 6 tells us, *Let him ask in faith, with no doubting.* The condition is that you must pray a prayer of faith. Why? Because doubt will destroy your ability to receive from God.

In verse 7, James goes so far as to say about the one who doubts, *let not that man suppose that he will receive **anything** from the Lord*. Why is this? Partly because doubt is something which shows God that we do not really trust Him. It has its roots in rebellion against God Himself. Another reason is because the one who doubts makes himself easy prey for the devil, who is then able to steal the answer to his prayer.

There is often a struggle involved in seeing prayers answered and the devil does whatever he can to delay or hinder it from coming. Although he cannot stop what God has said, he is able to hinder us from receiving it; and one of these hindrances is doubt. Doubt is a lack of conviction that what God has said is true. Doubt is believing what the circumstances and the current situation are saying. To doubt is to believe in something other than what God wants you to believe in.

Everyone believes in something, but God wants you to believe in what He says more than what anyone or anything else may be saying. God has designed it this way for a reason. He wants you to be able to *receive* and *keep* what He gives you. When you are in the spirit, walking in the spirit, walking in faith, you are unapproachable for the devil and he cannot get at you. 1 John 5:18 says, *...but he who has been born of God keeps himself, and the wicked one does not touch him*. We all know that the wicked one does indeed touch believers in an attempt to kill, steal, and destroy. But there is a place in the Spirit and a walk of faith which makes it impossible for him to get to you. You are protected and are able to receive from God.

Do Not Let Circumstances Rule You

Doubt causes you to be like a wave which is driven and tossed with the wind (James 1:6). If it feels good, then it *is* good. If people appreciate you, you are happy. If you experience hard times, you believe God has deserted you. If people are against you, you get depressed.

This is a sure sign that your trust is based in circumstances and people, and not in the Living God and His Word. You are like a wave; lacking stability, constantly dependant on external stimulation, a perpetual victim of circumstances. When someone asks you how you feel, you reply, "I'm fine, under the circumstances." In other words, the circumstances are over you and decide how you should be feeling. But God does not want you to be like this.

He does not want you to be a double-minded man, unstable in all your ways (James 1:8-9). He does not want insecurity and confusion to rule all that you do and every decision you make. He wants security, stability, and single-mindedness to rule and reign in your life.

How can this happen? It can never be accomplished by continuing to base your life on natural circumstances, but by connecting with the supernatural and believing the Word of God. In the external, in this natural world, there is nothing firm enough for you to stand on; but in the supernatural, there is a Rock, Jesus and His Word, which is immovable and unchanging, and will give your life all the stability it will ever need.

The Prayer of Faith

The prayer of faith is based on conviction regarding the will of God. It is therefore vital that you know His will before you pray. Many, many times we have prayed without believing, and have therefore received nothing from God (James 1:7).

When a need arises in your life, or you have something you want to ask of God, find out *first* what He says about it. This is something we miss far too often. We run to God in panic, and cry out, "God, do something, quick!" Then we look around us in despair and wonder, "Why didn't God do anything?" We walk away from Him in resignation and disappointment, and confusion because nothing happened. How many times does this take place in the believer's life!

Then we have all had teaching which says, "Perhaps it wasn't God's will to answer," "It's all for your own good," "Everything works together for good," or "The Lord works in mysterious ways."

This sort of teaching brings grief to the heart of God! God is not confused. His way is clear and straightforward, and He has a clear path for each one of us. He has answers to more questions in your life than you have ever thought, or anyone has ever told you.

Faith is also obedience (Romans 1:5), and God is depending on your coming to Him *in the way* He has prescribed. You have to come with the conviction that *He is a rewarder of those who diligently seek Him* (Hebrews 11:6). So there are certain things you need to do *before* you pray. You must first discover exactly *what* His will is. We cannot just skip over this step or leave it up to others to decide. You cannot let others direct or live your life for you. God wants to speak directly to you.

Someone came to me, once with a serious matter and asked for prayer. I asked if he had set aside a day to pray about the situation. He said, 'no.' Then I asked if he had taken a few hours or even *one* hour to pray and read the Word concerning God's will for his problem. The answer was still no! So I said, "There's no point in my praying for you, you just want me to solve the problem for you."

You are not meant to use the prayers of others as a way of escaping your own responsibility. Of course, we have to pray for one another and carry one another's burdens. But if you are not willing to take time with God and discover His will for yourself, you will never gain a personal conviction and you will remain an easy victim for the attacks of doubt, unbelief, fear, and contradictory circumstances. You need to do your homework and spend time in the Word so you know what God is saying to you personally. A conviction will then grow in your heart and you will be able to pray the prayer of faith.

If you have only one hour to spend with someone, it is better to spend fifty minutes in teaching and ten minutes in prayer, than the other way around. Prayer without conviction concerning God's will opens the door for confusion and attack.

So far, we have only been talking about the prayer of faith, a prayer based on the fact that you have seen and understood clearly the will of God.

The Prayer of Commitment in Relation to the Prayer of Faith
The prayer of commitment is relevant when you are unaware of God's will. It is a completely different type of prayer than the prayer of faith. Jesus prayed this kind of prayer in the Garden of Gethsemane when He committed His life into His Father's hands by saying, *Not as I will, but as You will.* Pray this prayer at those times when you need to commit your life and will to God so that His will can be accomplished.

You can also pray this prayer when you are unsure of God's will. For example, you may have two alternatives before you and are not sure which one to choose. Pray the prayer of commitment and ask for a revelation of God's will. Then when you have discovered His will, you no longer need to pray this prayer.

God's Word is His will. When you have seen His will in the Word, you can pray accordingly. You know what His will is. You do not need another revelation. What is written in the Bible applies to you, and you have a right to take hold of His promises and demand that they be fulfilled in your life. Why? Because Jesus died and with His blood paid the price for you to share in all that His promises contain.

You should not come to God just because you are in a desperate situation. It should not be your problem that rules you, but rather a conviction about the *solution*. God is moved primarily not by your needs, but by your faith. If He were moved by needs, the whole world would be saved, healed, and delivered today, but this is not the case. He is moved by faith. Those who call upon His name and believe in Him are saved. Romans 10:11-13 says,

For the Scripture says, "Whoever *believes* on Him will not be put to shame." For there is no distinction between Jew and Greek, for the same Lord over all is rich to all who call upon Him. For *"whoever calls upon the name of the Lord shall be saved."*

You should approach God with the conviction that He has the solution you need.

Let God be God

In this way, you can see the solution and not just the problem. You are convinced that *He is a rewarder of those who diligently seek Him* (Hebrews 11:6) So then, *when* you pray in that way, you know that He hears you. You are now praying the prayer of faith, with a conviction that your answer is on its way. You *know* that He will answer. You may not know how, when or in what way he will answer. But that is not your problem. It is God's problem.

It is not for you to decide *how* He will meet your needs. He has more and varied ways than you could ever imagine. It is not for you to decide *when* He will answer; but remember, God is never late. Neither is it for you to decide through *whom* He will answer; it is of no consequence to you. God is not a respecter of persons, and neither should you be.

This is where many people have gone wrong. Perhaps they may have prayed for revival in their city, but when it came it was in a different way to what they had imagined and through people other than those they had thought God would use. So they are filled with anger and even go so far as to work against what they themselves had prayed for! Why? Because even before they prayed, they had made up their minds as to *how* revival would come, and through *whom* it would come (they usually have themselves in mind).

Never try to restrict God in this way. He is not as limited as you think! Do what He has told you to do—pray, and let God do His part—bring the answer. Do not play the part of the Holy Spirit by supervising or trying to orchestrate the answer. God is much better at it than we are!

Cast your cares upon Him instead, knowing that He cares for you (1 Peter 5:7). You do not need to worry about the answer when you *know* He is watching over you. However, if you do not believe in your heart that He cares for you, you will begin to worry and try to sort things out by yourself. By doing this you are standing in the way of God taking your problem and turning it into a miracle.

Philippians 4:6-7 says,

Be anxious for nothing, but in *everything* by prayer and supplication, with thanksgiving, let your requests be made known to God; and the peace of God, which surpasses all understanding, will guard your hearts and minds through Christ Jesus.

If you make your prayers and requests known to God and cast your cares on Him, His peace will keep you. How? By the knowledge that He actually does take your cares and hears you when you pray, that He *will and can* answer your prayers, and that they will indeed be answered. Your mind is kept in perfect peace, even when it is beyond your understanding as to how, when, and through whom your answer will come.

See Your Answer with the Eyes of Faith
*Whatever you ask for in prayer, **believe that you have received it**, and it **will** be yours* (Mark 11:24 NIV). When should you believe that you

have received what you asked for? When you see the answer? When everything feels good? When everything finally works out? No, you are to believe when you *pray*!

You believe while the problem is still there and the answer is completely invisible. While the mountain still looms before you, you believe that you *have already* received. You receive in faith even before you see the answer, though at the same time you can indeed see your answer with the eyes of faith.

Remember that faith is *the evidence of things not seen* (Hebrews 11:1). You see it as visible before it becomes visible and you believe you have it before you see it. Jesus says, when you believe that it is yours before you see it, it *shall* be yours.

This is what Abraham did. His did not look at his nearly dead body. Instead, he kept his eyes on the promise and knew that since God had promised him a son he would have a son—and a son is what he got! God kept His Word to Abraham and He will do the same for you!

When you can pray and believe that you have received before you actually see anything, you do not need to continue praying thirty-two times for the same thing, as though you were desperately trying to persuade God to meet your need. God is not a mean, greedy or double-minded God who needs to be persuaded into helping you. Matthew 7:11 says,

How much more will your Father who is in heaven give *good things* to those who *ask Him*!

God is more willing to answer your prayers in an abundant way than you are to come to Him in prayer. He does not need to be convinced—it is you who need to let yourself be!

After you have prayed the prayer of faith, the Word has gone out and begun to work and your answer is on its way. You do not need to pray to God about it any more, you can begin to thank Him for what is coming. Why? Because 1 John 5:14-15 says,

Now this is the confidence that we have in Him, that if we ask *anything according to His will*, He hears us. And if we know that He hears us, *whatever* we ask, we know that *we already have* the petitions that we have asked of Him.

Speak the Solution—Instead of the Problem

This is a tremendous revelation! If you know that what you are asking for is in accordance with His will (something you know when you are praying in accordance with His Word and thus fulfilling the conditions of the promise), you can also know that you *already have* what you asked for. When? Even before you see it!

If you already know that it is yours, you do not need to pray about it any more. If you do, your prayer will eventually become one of unbelief, indicating you are not certain that you have what you prayed for or are going to receive it. Doubt has entered in, and you have become the kind of person James is referring to when he says, *For let not that man suppose that he will receive anything from the Lord; he is a double-minded man, unstable in all his ways* (James 1:7-8).

If you have already received the answer to your prayer, you must trust that it will come. You should begin to thank God that it is on the way. Then confess the Word of God over your situation. Say what God says about your circumstances, not what your circumstances try to say about God! Speak the solution instead of the problem. Use the weapons God has given you to resist the devil. Attack and put pressure on him, and make him unable to hinder or delay your answer from coming.

This is the struggle that sometimes makes it necessary to "pray things through." There is nothing standing between you and God;

you do not need to pray through to get to Him. He says that you have *boldness to enter the Holiest by the blood of Jesus* (Hebrews 10:19), and that we can *come boldly to the throne of grace, that we may obtain mercy and find grace to help in time of need* (Hebrews 4:16). Through the blood of Jesus, the way has been opened to the throne of God.

This had great significance for a Jew who had been taught about the holiness of God's throne. The Holy of Holies was inaccessible for all but the High Priest, who himself was allowed to enter just once a year. No one else knew what was inside or was allowed to go in. Those who tried to do so would die. But now, through the blood of Jesus, God tells us that *anyone can come at any time* to receive *whatever* they need, and to "find grace to help in time of need."

The revelation that God is willing to help, hear, and respond to everyone, and that the Gospel contains *everything* for *everyone* in *every* situation shakes the devil's kingdom. He takes great pains to hide the revelation that the Gospel covers everything, *whatever* our need might be. One of his tactics is to make prayer appear complicated and incomprehensible and to have us thinking it is almost impossible to get God to answer us. This, of course, is not the case.

We do not need to "pray through" to God. The way to Him is open and free. We need to pray through the spirit realm, resisting principalities and powers and holding our ground as we stand on the Word. The victory will be ours when we hold on to what God has said and use the weapons He has given us. God longs to answer every one of our prayers, for when we bear much fruit He will be greatly glorified (John 15:7-8).

9

Faith for Healing

*When evening had come, they brought to Him many who were demon-possessed. And He cast out the spirits with a word, and healed **all** who were sick, that it might be fulfilled which was spoken by Isaiah the prophet, saying: "He Himself took our infirmities and bore our sicknesses"* (Matthew 8:16-17).

(The 1981 version of the Swedish Bible says, ...lifted our sicknesses from off us). The faith we have comes from Jesus. It is a supernatural gift which enables us to believe in Him.

He is the author and perfector of our faith and it is Him we should look to. But not only is He the author or initiator of our faith, He is also the One who increases and perfects it. And He does this by exhorting us to keep our eyes fixed on Him (Hebrews 12:2). But how do we keep our eyes fixed on Him? By looking at who He is, what He has accomplished for us on the Cross, what He did as He walked here on earth. What He is doing today as He is seated at the right hand of the Father in heaven, and what He is doing on earth today through those who believe in Him. If we get a firm conviction of all of that, then we are looking at Jesus.

When we look at Jesus as He walked on earth, it is obvious that much of what He did consisted of healing the sick. In fact, at least one third of all His time in ministry was spent healing the sick.

When Peter preached to the Gentiles in the house of Cornelius in Acts 10:38, he said that *Jesus went about **doing good** and healing all who were oppressed by the devil, for God was with Him*. Wherever Jesus met sick people He healed them. It was an important part of His ministry—not something He pushed to one side, minimised or tried to explain away. Acts 10:38 says that He *went about doing good, and healing all*. Healing is good. It comes from heaven and is the will of God.

Hebrews 13:8 tells us that *Jesus Christ is the same yesterday, today, and forever.* In other words, as Jesus was when He walked on earth, so He is today, and so will He be for eternity. He never changes, nor does He stop what He was doing. He is consistent: He does not break His promises, and His character and works are unchangeable. What He did when He walked on earth, He is still doing today! This is good news; the news of the Gospel.

What did Jesus do while He was on earth? He taught, He preached, He trained Hus disciples, He forgave sins, He healed the sick, and He cast out devils. He has not changed. He is exactly the same today.

By doing these things He proclaimed the Kingdom of God, because it is just those things that proclaim the Kingdom of God! God's Kingdom is not an abstract concept which no one is capable of understanding. God's Kingdom is tangible and concrete. Where God's Kingdom is made manifest, people are restored and delivered. Demons are cast out, the sick are healed, people begin to walk in faith and follow Jesus, and the power of God is revealed.

God Wants to Heal Everyone

If Jesus healed the sick while He was on earth, then He heals the sick today! Why? Because Jesus came to earth to do the will of God (Hebrews 10:7). He did not come to do the things He thought would be nice or fun. He did not come to show everyone what a great anointing He had. He came to fully reveal *who* God is and *what* God's will is. Jesus *is* the will of God.

Everything Jesus said and *everything* Jesus did was automatically the will of the Father. In John 5:19 Jesus said:

The Son can do nothing of Himself, but what He sees the Father do; for whatever He does, the Son also does in like manner.

If Jesus healed someone who was sick, it meant that the Father did the same, and it was God's will. Jesus is God's will revealed to us. That gives us hope for today. If Jesus is the same today as He was back then, and if Jesus is the will of God revealed, then it must be God's will to heal today. And so it is! Healing is from heaven, it is good and it is the will of God!

But the question then comes, "So, does God want to heal everyone?" What this question *really* means is, "Does God want to heal *me*?"

"If God wants to heal everyone, there's a chance He wants to heal me. But, if He doesn't want to heal everybody, then it's not absolutely certain that He wants to heal exactly me. If He doesn't want to heal absolutely everybody, well maybe I'm in the group of people He doesn't want to heal. So if I ask for healing and I just happen to be in the category which He doesn't want to heal, then I can't pray with boldness and I can't be sure of receiving an answer. So it's hard to pray in faith"

This is the position that many people have gotten themselves into when praying for healing. They have found themselves in a no-man's land of insecurity, thinking, "Maybe God wants to heal me, maybe He doesn't. Perhaps He's got some hidden purpose for not wanting to heal me. Maybe this sickness is from Him to train me for eternity," and so on.

If a whole bunch of these thoughts and ideas plague us as we pray, we will not be able to pray in faith, nor will we receive an answer, according to James 1:6-8. Faith begins only where the will of God is known. We need to know the will of God before we pray, otherwise we will be attacked by doubt and contradictory circumstances and be unable to receive what God has for us. We give up and say, "I guess it just wasn't God's will", long before the answer has been given a chance to manifest.

The manifestation of an answer to prayer, healing included, can take time. Not all healing happens immediately, but by no means does this mean that it is not on the way. To be able to receive and hold on to healing, however, I have to know the will of God! The question is, does God want to heal everybody?—in other words, does He want to heal *exactly* me!

We would all agree that God *is able* to heal. Even an atheist would acknowledge this by saying, "Well, if God does exist, He obviously has the ability to do anything, including the ability to heal the sick!" We believe that God does exist, and therefore that He *is able* to heal. But that is not enough. The question is, does He want to! When you get a personal conviction that the Lord does indeed want to heal you, then you will be in the right position to be able to receive from Him.

Jesus Healed All Those Who Came to Him

How, then, can we tell whether or not God wants to heal? By looking at Jesus! What did He do? *He went about doing good and healing all who were oppressed by the devil, for God was with Him* (Acts 10:38). Everywhere there were sick people, they came to Jesus; and when they did, He healed every sickness and every disease among them (Matt 9:35, 12:15, 14:14, 35-36, 15:30-31; Mark 6:56; Luke 6:19, 9:11, and more). Luke 9:11 tells us that Jesus *healed those who had need of healing*. When the need arose, He provided healing.

110

Wherever Jesus went, those who came to Him were healed. Someone might say, "But He didn't heal everyone in Israel, so we shouldn't go and empty all the hospitals, should we?" No, Jesus only healed those who *came* to Him. Not everyone in the hospital will come to Jesus; not everyone believes in the healing power of God. But when people *came to hear Him, and be healed of their diseases...power went out from Him and healed them all* (Luke 6:17, 19).

Nowhere in the Bible, do you find Jesus saying 'No' to anyone. You will never find Jesus telling a sick person who has come to Him, "I can't heal you," or "It's not the right time for you to be healed" or "God wants you to keep your illness so He can be glorified." When was God glorified? When Jesus performed miracles—such as when Lazarus was raised from the dead! (John 11:4, 40-44).

You never see Jesus going around saying, "In the name of God, be sick." He never dealt out diseases to people as though they were blessings. Sickness is not a blessing. On the contrary, Jesus was moved with compassion for the multitudes because they were weary and scattered, like sheep having no shepherd (Matt 9:36). That is why He healed them.

You will never see Jesus turn away someone who is sick. He did not say, "I could heal you, but I don't want to." It would have been more merciful for Him to have said, "I'd like to heal you, but I can't." Many people see God as fundamentally *able* to do something but hardly *willing* to do it. They see His will as something incomprehensible and hidden. But this is completely wrong!

God is exactly as He has revealed Himself to be in Jesus. Jesus is *the brightness of His glory and the express image of His person* (Hebrews 1:3). God is precisely the way He has revealed Himself through the Bible and the life of Jesus, not in the least bit different. He has not revealed one will through Jesus and the Bible, while reserving another will which is secret, unstable, and cannot be understood. God is more than the Bible, He is more than His promises, but He is *no different* from the person Jesus has revealed. God does not want us to call into question His ability, which is immeasurable, but less still does He want you question His loving will as revealed in His Son.

A leper once came to Jesus saying, *Lord, if You are willing, You can make me clean.* The question of God's willingness was answered once and for all when Jesus replied, *I am willing; be cleansed* (Matthew 8:2-3). God had already said His "I will" and Jesus demonstrated this by healing all those who came to Him. Why? Because He was anointed by the Spirit for this very purpose! Why? Because healing is good! Why? Because healing is available to everybody! Why? Because God was with Him! He *went about doing good and healing all who were oppressed by the devil, for God was with Him* (Acts 10:38).

Do Not Let Your Reason or Experiences Hold You Back

Now that you have seen that healing is available to everyone, you can believe that it is available to *you* as well. A Scriptural conviction that God wants to heal you is beginning to grow. As you meditate seriously on what the Word of God says about healing, though, you should be aware that the devil will bombard you with a host of theological arguments and or negative experiences.

Throughout the Church's history, there have always been two great enemies of divine revelation: rationalism and empiricism. More simply put, they are reason and experience, both of which raise up thoughts and imaginations that are contrary to the Word of God. Reason says, "I can't understand it, so I don't accept it." While experiential thinking says, "I've never experienced this before, we've never done it this way before, so I don't accept it." You must learn to resist both of these thought patterns.

Miracles are real, whether you have experienced them or not. When it comes to healing, you cannot judge what is right or wrong based on your experience, be it positive or negative. You cannot say, "I don't believe God wants to heal everyone because my aunt didn't get better", or "I believe God wants to heal everyone because my knee got healed." You do not believe God on the basis of what you have or have not experienced, but on the basis of what He has said in His Word, whether you have seen it or not. God is who He has said He is, and He does what He has said He will do, whether you have seen it or not. Your stepping-off point must be what God has said stands and that He *is going to do* what He has promised to do. That is why you cannot afford to let negative experiences, whether they be your own or others, take from you all that God has promised in His Word.

The Holy Spirit is a gentleman when it comes to the experiences of others. He does not gossip about reasons why healing might not have taken place. Nor does He tell you about the situations others may be in. God wants you to seek Him regarding your *own* situation and receive what He has for you in His Word.

Jesus Came to Restore the Whole Man

Look to Jesus, He reveals God's will. He forgave people's sins and healed them. We have often divided up the things that God keeps together. When God created man, He created him as an entity. No single part is insignificant. No single part should be despised. When man fell in sin, he did so completely; spirit, soul, and body. Not a single part of his being escaped the corruption of the Fall, the body included.

When Jesus came, He came to restore the whole of man, not just some parts. The redemption He has provided includes man's entire being and not just his spirit. God is no less interested in man's body than He is in man's soul or spirit. He created the whole man. There is, of course, no doubt that above all else, the most important thing is that a person's spirit be born again, enabling him to go to heaven. There is nothing more important than being saved and escaping hell and eternal separation from God. But this does not mean that God places the new birth in opposition to bodily healing. You do not have to choose. God has provided for your salvation at every level. When Jesus died on the Cross, He took the sin of mankind upon Himself, but He also carried our diseases (Isaiah 53:4,5). He paid our debt in full. He took our anguish so we could have peace. He was made sin that we might have His righteousness, and by His stripes we are healed.

Psalm 103:2-3 says,

Bless the Lord, O my soul, and *forget not* all His benefits: Who forgives *all* your iniquities, Who heals *all* your *diseases*.

To the man sick with palsy in Mark chapter 2, Jesus said, *Son, your sins are forgiven you, and Arise take up your bed, and go your way to your house* (Mark 2:5, 11). Jesus both forgave him and healed him. Why? Because both forgiveness of sins and bodily healing are included in our redemption. Salvation covers the whole man.

As we have seen before, the word saved, or salvation, is the Greek word '*sozo*,' meaning both salvation and healing. It is sometimes used in the New Testament to refer to deliverance from sin and sometimes to mean healing from sickness. Why? Because salvation includes both!

God Would Never Despise Your Body—It is His Temple
Early in the history of the Church, gnosticism and Platonic thought began to strongly influence Christian doctrine. Signs and wonders became less frequent and a contempt for the body and what is physical crept in. Monasticism and asceticism became a means of

reaching God and making oneself worthy of salvation. The great truth that everything had been accomplished and finished on the Cross was forgotten. Self-denial and mortification of the physical body were believed to release the spirit and spiritual life. This, however, is not Christianity. It is nothing more than gnosticism and Greek philosophy.

God has never despised what He created. His creation is not evil, it is good. When He had finished creating, He looked at the result of His work and saw that *it was very good* (Genesis 1:31). For this reason, through the redemption completed by Jesus on the Cross, God has provided complete salvation for man as a whole; his spirit, his soul, and his body.

The human body is precious. It is a temple for God's Spirit and God's glory, and God is interested in, and has a plan for this part of a person, just as much as He has for his spirit (1 Corinthians 6:19-20). Sickness is not God's will, as much as sin is not His will. The will of God is forgiveness and healing. Sickness does not come from God. The ultimate source of sickness is the devil.

Before the Fall, sickness did not exist. Sickness came into the world through the devil's seducing man to sin, and since then it has been present in this world. Sickness does not exist in heaven, and we will no longer know it when we get there. Jesus never talks about sickness as though it were from God. On the contrary, Acts 10:38 says that Jesus *went about doing good and healing all who were oppressed by the devil*. Sickness is the devil's attack on the human body. In Luke 13:16 Jesus says,

So ought not this woman, being a daughter of Abraham, whom Satan has bound for eighteen years, be loosed from this bond on the Sabbath?

Jesus calls sickness a bond and not a blessing, and His job was to *proclaim liberty to the captives* (Luke 4:18). He says that Satan, not

God, had kept her in bondage, and that God's will was to set her free and heal her. If Jesus says that sickness is from the devil, He means exactly that. This does not mean that every sick person is demon-possessed or under the influence of the evil one. Nor does it mean, as has been wrongly interpreted by some, that a sick person is somehow evil or malicious.

An unsaved person who happens to be sick is just like any other unsaved person according to the Bible; their heart—not their health—determines their true state. A Christian who belongs to God is His beloved child and completely accepted by God. Neither sickness nor health are criteria for inclusion in God's family, or for being loved and accepted by Him. When the Bible talks about healing, it does not do so to belittle anyone, because Jesus wants to give His life and His power to every one of us, wherever our need may be.

The Gospel and God's willingness to heal have been said by some to show "contempt for the weak." How completely wrong! If this were the case, Jesus despised the weak more than anyone since He was always ready to heal the sick. Jesus brought the power of God to the weak and the sick in order to heal and deliver them—something He continues to do even today. When we teach on healing we see it as an expression of Jesus' compassion. It demonstrates how He is moved for people and how much He desires to heal them.

"Yes, but that was Jesus," you might say. "Nothing ever happens nowadays. No one ever gets healed in our church!" Does anyone expect to be healed in your church? Do people pray for the sick expecting Jesus to actually heal them? Is there any teaching on what the Bible says about healing? Or are people ashamed of the Gospel and spend their time explaining it away?

Preach Healing—And There Will be Healing
Not even Jesus can heal the sick in an atmosphere of unbelief in Him. The Gospel must be heard and received in faith before it can

become the power of God to salvation. When Jesus came to His home town of Nazareth, *He could do no mighty work there, except that He laid His hands on a few sick people and healed them. And He marvelled because of their unbelief* (Mark 6:5-6).

The same thing happens today. Jesus comes to many places where He is able to do very little. He wants to perform miracles, but He cannot. Notice that the Scripture tells us He could not do any mighty work. No matter how much He wanted to, He just could not. Why not? Because of their unbelief, in spite of the fact that He was God's own Son, anointed with the power of the Holy Spirit. He was limited by their unbelief. It is precisely the same today: reluctance, rebellion, scepticism, and unbelief stop God's power from working miracles.

Why do you find it so easy to receive forgiveness for your sins? Because you have heard a lot of teaching from the Word about forgiveness. When you get to hear just as much about another side of your redemption, that *by His stripes you are healed*, then healing and miracles will become more natural for you, and it will be easier for the Spirit of God to perform signs and wonders and heal the sick.

How is it then that you receive healing? Just like you receive everything else from God—by faith! It is by faith that you receive what He has done for you on the Cross concerning your health. By the stripes of Jesus you have been given healing. You see that He has already taken your sickness on the Cross and that health is available to you right now.

God's healing power to come to you in many different ways: through the prayer of faith, by the laying on of hands, by being anointed with oil, through a prayer cloth, through the Lord's Supper, by a manifestation of one of the gifts of the Spirit, or through the Word of God which heals. God has a wealth of different ways to convey His healing power to you. But no matter where you are, you can always receive your healing by faith on the basis of your redemption and the promises of the covenant. The relevant Scripture is Mark 11:23,-24. If you believe that what you say will come to pass, then you will have what you say.

Remember, healing does not always manifest immediately. The body may still be under attack for a long period of time, but you should still consider that your healing is an accomplished fact through the work of Jesus. Because of what the Word of God says, you know your healing will come to pass. You can rest in this conviction and let the Word of God and the Spirit of God work the complete healing in your body. You do not need to 'prove' anything by throwing away your medicine, refusing to see the doctor, or taking similarly foolish steps in an attempt to be a "faith person."

God is in no way opposed to doctors or medicine. They are also His tools in fighting a common enemy. When your healing is manifested, then you do not need your medicine any longer, nor do you need to go to the doctor any more. Until that day comes, however, do not let anyone push you into doing something that simply is not necessary.

You do not have to prove anything to anyone. Just walk in faith, believing that God *wants* to heal you and that healing *has* been provided for you on the Cross. Continue to walk in faith that you received healing when you prayed, or when someone else prayed for you, laid their hands on you or anointed you with oil, etc. You can go with a quiet confidence that the power of God is working complete healing in your body and that sickness must leave in the name of Jesus.

The Word of God carries you, the Holy Spirit comforts and guides you, Jesus is the author and finisher of your faith. He is your health, He is *the* LORD *who heals you* (Exodus 15:26). The more you fix your eyes on Him, the greater your expectancy, and the more freedom He will have to work a miracle in your life.

10

Faith for Abundance

God is the God of abundance. His covenant name is, "El Shaddai," the God who is more than enough. More than enough for all your needs. He is the One *who is able to do exceedingly abundantly above all that we ask or think, according to the power that works in us* (Ephesians 3:20). God is infinite, His resources are inexhaustible, His ability is immense—and He has made Himself available to you!

God created the world, we did not. He created the mountains, the rivers, and the heavens, we did not. But He did it for us. He created everything in order to put man, made in His own image, in its midst. He created the earth as a place where man could be, where he could serve God, love God, glorify God, enjoy fellowship with God and be His co-worker. Psalm 115:16 says, *The heaven, even the heavens, are the Lord's; But the earth He has given to the children of men.*

God Gives of His Abundance

When God created Adam and Eve, they had no poverty nor any deficiency in any area of their lives. God is the God of abundance, and out of His abundant life He gave them all they needed and more. Philippians 4:19 tells us, *And my God shall supply all your need according to His riches in glory by Christ Jesus.* God is a rich God who met Adam and Eve's every need in abundance. He placed them in a beautiful garden, not out in a desert somewhere to discipline them.

He called the garden Eden which is a Hebrew word meaning "richness, abundance, and delight." Why did God give the Garden this particular name? Because He intended for man to live in and enjoy abundance in every area of life.

What then is abundance? *Abundance is having more than we need for ourselves so that we can give to others and meet their needs as well.*

Some people think abundance only applies to money or material possessions, but that is not the case. It applies to our time, energy, interests, our love, health, wisdom and knowledge—the total sphere of our lives. God's abundant life covers everything—every area of our being. God is like that. He has an overflow out of which He is constantly giving. He is love and love is always giving, it does not take, it gives. God gave His best, most generous gift, He gave His Son.

God is a generous giver, who uses everything He has to meet mankind's every need. His nature is like that, and it is that nature that we received a part of when we were born again.

Before sin came into the world, poverty and deficiency were non-existent. They came as a result of sin and its curse. This is extremely important to understand. Poverty and need do not come as blessings from God, but rather they are a curse from the devil, through sin. The devil is a thief who steals, kills, and destroys (John 10:10). He is continually robbing man. God is continually giving. When the curse of sin came over the world, need was one of its consequences. Poverty is a curse, not a blessing. Starvation, want, unpaid bills, and debt are not blessings; they are misery. They did not exist before the Fall, nor was it God's will that man should have to suffer them!

We are in Covenant With God

After the Fall, when God began speaking with Abraham, He called him and blessed him. This blessing was passed on as an inheritance to cover the whole nation of Israel. It was a blessing that applied to every area of life, the financial area included.

God was preparing the way for humanity to return to its original position of fellowship and abundant life, which had been forfeited through the Fall. That is why God picked Abraham out, so that through him He could form a people through whom the Messiah would come, He who would bless the whole world. God set Abraham apart and blessed him so that he would become a blessing to all humanity and a father of many nations (Genesis 12:1-3, 17:1-8). God made a covenant with Abraham, and Abraham walked in faith before his God.

A covenant involves two partners. In this instance, the God who is more than enough (Genesis 17:1) took the initiative. Entering into a covenant means placing all that you are, all that you have, and all that you can do at the disposal of the other party. A covenant requires faithfulness and commitment at every level from both partners. We have heard plenty of teaching about how important it is that we commit ourselves to God. And that it is, but we have often overlooked the results of making such a commitment. When one member of a covenant commits himself to another, everything he has is placed at the disposal of the other.

When God entered into covenant with Abraham, He expected his complete devotion in faith. All that Abraham had in his spirit, soul, and body, in every area of his life, he placed at God's disposal.

This is actually what we do when we confess Jesus as Lord of our lives. We commit ourselves to Him entirely. We desire to serve, follow, and glorify Him rather than ourselves. If He wants to use our time, it is at His disposal. If He requires our talents, they are available to Him. If He wants to use our hands to be laid on the sick, our feet to carry the Gospel, our mouth to preach, or our money and possessions to finance the Gospel, He can, since they all belong to Him through the covenant. All that we have belongs to Him, because He is our Lord and we have committed ourselves to Him. We are no longer our own, we have been bought with a price (1 Corinthians 6:19-20).

All of God's Resources Have
Become Ours Through the Covenant

Commitment is the prerequisite for the Christian life. It is a prerequisite to God's abundant life and promises being made available to us. But we have often stopped there and that is not what God wants. He wants our motives to be pure so that we live wholeheartedly for Him, not selfishly in the short-lived pleasure of sin. Rather than seeking our own good, we seek first His Kingdom.

In Matthew 6:33 Jesus says, *But seek first the kingdom of God and His righteousness, and **all these things** shall be added to you.* What are all these things Jesus is referring to? He has just finished talking about food and clothing (Matthew 6:25-32), telling us not to worry about such things. He says, *For after all these things the Gentiles seek. For your heavenly Father knows that you need all these things* (Matthew 6:32). God is aware of our every need in every area of our lives, including our food, clothing, housing, etc. He is also aware of our financial needs. God has something to give on every level.

A covenant involves mutual commitment. We give our lives to God and place all that we have at His disposal. But at the same time, God commits Himself to us fully and places all that He is, all that He has, and all that He is able to do at our disposal. The partners in a covenant are obliged to stand up for each other, to respond to each other's needs and to help one another. God has taken the initiative and entered into such a covenant with us. He has personally chosen an obligation to support and help us. He wants us to bring our needs before Him and watch Him meet them miraculously.

This is why David was able to say, *The Lord is my shepherd; I shall not want* (Psalms 23:1). In accordance with His covenant, God has abundantly provided us with all that He has through Christ Jesus. He is like the father in the parable of the prodigal son who said, *Son, you are always with me, and **all that I have is yours*** (Luke 15:31).

Christians always had difficulty accepting God's blessing in the area of finances. Throughout the years, gnostic thinking based on Greek philosophy rather than Biblical revelation has crept into the Church. This way of thinking harbours contempt for the material and physical world while exalting that which is 'spiritual.' Gnosticism disdains the material and is totally unscriptural!

God looked at the material world He had created and called it *good* (Genesis 1:4, 10, 12, 18, 21, 25, 31). In fact, God says seven times that what He created is good. Why? Because He knew the devil would attack His creation and deceive us into believing that it is evil and must be avoided.

However, we are not to try to escape creation. We have been created to use it, enjoy it, and preserve it rather than despise what God has made.

God placed us in a material world and this is where we are to glorify Him. When God blessed Abraham and Israel in the Old Covenant, He blessed them on every level. He blessed them with camels, donkeys, servants, gold, possessions, lands, streams of water, victory in battle, and so on (Genesis 13:2; Deuteronomy 28:1-14). Even as Israel left Egypt, they carried with them the gold and silver of the Egyptians.

Money—A Means of Spreading the Gospel

For Abraham, riches were not a hindrance to serving God, rather as a means of doing so. God is not opposed to wealth, He is against a greedy and self-centred heart. The root of all evil is not money, it is the *love* of money, (1 Timothy 6:9, 10). The real sin is one of lust, and when this is done away with, material possessions can become an effective means for God to spread His Gospel in the world. "Yes, but didn't Jesus tell the rich young ruler to go and sell all that he owned before he could follow Him?" Of course He did, and when the rich young man heard this he was grieved and *went away sorrowful, for he had great possessions* (Mark 10:22). Then Jesus said, *How hard it is for those who trust in riches to enter the kingdom of God!* (Mark 10:23).

It might appear as though money and possessions do nothing but cause problems and make it difficult to follow Jesus. But this is not the case! The rich young man's problem was not that he had many possessions, but that his many possessions had him. This is why he went away saddened and grieved. You will always be sad when you have to leave something you love, and the rich young ruler obviously loved his money more than he loved Jesus. You cannot love both God and money, but you can serve God with your possessions.

Luke 8:3 talks about the group of women who followed Jesus and his disciples and helped *support them out of their own means* (Luke 8:3 NIV). They had not left all they had to follow Jesus. Instead, they followed Jesus and served Him with all that they owned. If you do not have anything, then you have nothing to give. God is not against your owning things—He is against things owning you.

As we continue to read about the rich young ruler, we see that the disciples began to wonder who could be saved if it was so difficult for a rich man to enter the Kingdom of God. This is where we often fail to grasp the whole context. Jesus answered their questions by using what had just taken place to teach them about material possessions (Mark 10:24-31). Peter commented, *See, we have left all and followed You.* Jesus responded by saying, ***There is no one*** *who has left house or brothers or sisters or father or mother or wife or children or lands, for My sake, and the gospel's,* ***who shall not receive a hundredfold now in this time****—houses and brothers and sisters and mothers and children and lands, with persecutions—and in the age to come, eternal life.*

What is Jesus really saying here? He is saying that if you commit all that you have to Him, and maintain an attitude of freedom which allows you to forsake things when necessary for the expansion of His Kingdom, you will *receive a* ***hundredfold*** *now in this time.* If you are committed to God, then He is a hundred times more committed to you and ready to abundantly meet your every need, including the material ones. If the rich young ruler had understood this, he would gladly have given away all that he owned.

Give and it Will be Given to You

The knowledge that God always gives in return will make you a cheerful giver who does not need to desparately cling onto possessions because of greed and fear. Then you will be able to give what God wants you to give, because you know that according to the covenant, God will always take care of you and supply you with more than enough. In Luke 6:38 Jesus says,

Give, and it will be given to you: good measure, pressed down, shaken together, and running over will be put into your bosom. For with the same measure that you use, it will be measured back to you.

The key to this is commitment and obedience. Be willing to give. Be quick to give. This will result in what Jesus has promised, *it will be given to you*. The return He promises is abundant, *good measure, pressed down, shaken together, and running over.*

God gives a return on whatever you give. Some people may say, "But isn't it selfish to give just to receive?" You are not giving just to get something back. You are giving because God wants you to and because love makes you want to meet the needs of others. However, when you give you will receive. This is a law which always works. Jesus Himself said it. He said, *Give, and it will be given to you*. This is the law of sowing and reaping. It applies to every area of life, finances included.

Paul talks about this in 2 Corinthians 9:6 when he says, *But this I say: He who sows sparingly will also reap sparingly, and he who sows bountifully will also reap bountifully.* Paul is actually talking about money in this instance. He is instructing the Corinthians regarding a collection, and in doing so he is applying the law of sowing and reaping.

Then in verse 10, he likens our money and belongings to seed, which can be sown. When a farmer plants seed, he actually believes there will be a harvest. There is nothing wrong with believing you will get a harvest from what you sow! The harvest is always greater than what was originally sown, making it possible for you to go on sowing even more and blessing others even more.

When you sow, you do not get poorer, you get richer.

The world tells you, "Put it away for a rainy day," but God says, "Give and you will receive." Proverbs 11:24 says, *There is one who scatters, yet increases more; And there is one who withholds more than is right, but it leads to poverty.* There is a spiritual law that says you have to sow to be able to reap. Sowing from what you own means that first you need to have something to sow, but that you do not greedily demand to keep it all for yourself.

For this reason Paul says, in 2 Corinthians 9:11, *You will be **made rich in every way** so that you can be generous on every occasion* (NIV). Why would Paul tell the Corinthians that they would be made rich if it is a sin to be rich? Because it is not a sin to be rich! It was the rich young ruler's greed and lust for money that was the sin, not the possessions themselves. When Paul exhorts those who are rich, in 1 Timothy 6:17-18, he does not tell them to give away everything they own and live ascetically in sackcloth and ashes and escape the material world. He tells them instead not to *trust in uncertain riches but in the living God, who gives us richly all things to enjoy.* He also tells them to be *ready to give, willing to share*.

In other words, we should not place a false trust in our wallets, bank accounts, stocks, or bonds because they are uncertain. The wind might be in our favour one day, but it could be against us the next. No, our hope instead, should be in God, who will never leave us or forsake us because He is the God of covenant. We can enjoy all that He has richly given us and share what we have to bless others and support the Lord's work. Then the Gospel will have the finances it needs to reach the uttermost ends of the earth.

11

Impediments to Faith

Faith releases the power of God and makes it available here on earth. Unbelief stops it from flowing. For this reason the devil attacks faith and the teaching of faith as much as possible, knowing that unbelief will prevent God from becoming a manifest reality to mankind.

When the Word is preached in the power of the Holy Spirit, it is confirmed with signs and wonders (Mark 16:20). These signs and wonders are what God uses to draw people to Jesus. He does this with what the Bible calls His "glory and miracle working power" (2 Peter 1:3, Swedish translation).

The devil is opposed to this glory and miracle working power affecting unbelievers in any way whatsoever. So he attacks faith so that signs and wonders shall not be released through faith. If he can hold back faith, he can hold back the salvation and deliverance of many.

The Bible talks about a variety of impediments to faith which have to be taken away before the power of God can be released. Unanswered prayers are often a result of one or more of these impediments, and until it is removed, we can go on praying indefinitely and still see no results.

Impediment 1: Unawareness That You Already Have Faith

The first impediment is, quite simply, a lack of awareness that you already have faith—something we have already spoken about. So long as you believe you are lacking in faith, you will be unable to avail yourself of the promises that apply to you as a believer. So long as you believe you need to have some sort of special faith to see God do miracles, and that only a select few ever receive it, you will never personalise the promises of God. But in John 14:12 Jesus says, *he who believes in Me, the works that I do he will do also* (notice that Jesus is talking about the individual and not the collective faith of the Church); *and greater works than these he will do*. According to Jesus, the individual believer is *supposed* to do what He did.

If you are a believer, you have faith (Romans 12:3). You do not need to pray for something you already have. Rather than doubting and disbelieving what has been given to you, put it to work. Your faith may not have the capacity for great miracles right away, but it will grow in strength. In 2 Thessalonians 1:3 Paul thanks God that their "faith grows exceedingly."

Impediment 2: Ignorance of God's Will

The second impediment to your faith is an ignorance of God's will. Faith is only active where the will of God is known. If there is any area in your life, about which or within which you do not know what God's will is, your faith cannot be active or operational in that place. In the book of Philemon verse 6, Paul prays that, *you may be active in sharing your faith, so that you will have a full understanding of every good thing we have in Christ* (NIV). If there is somewhere in your life where you do not understand "every good thing we have in Christ," you will not avail yourself of the good things He has for you. Faith makes a withdrawal from what has been deposited as your inheritance. You will not make a withdrawal, however, if you are unaware of the fact that there is something in your account.

For hundreds of years the devil has been working overtime to keep us ignorant of this fact. If you do not comprehend the true meaning of reconciliation, or what Jesus has accomplished for you and made available to you, or the contents of the inheritance you have received, you will never make use of them. God calls you His child, son, heir, fellow-worker, king and priest. The devil calls you wretched, poor, worthless and a failure.

Ignorance of who God says you *are* and what His Word says you *have* will hold you in bondage and defeat.

As in the days of Gideon when the Midianites took every single weapon and piece of iron from Israel, the devil has taken God's promises and revelation from the believers, making them unable to defend themselves against his attacks. We have often heard examples of how 'on-fire' Christians have become ill and later died. Then people sometimes say, "Do you mean to say that so-and-so didn't have faith? He prayed, and look at what happened—he died."

It is important to understand when this sort of thing happens that, first, we have no right to judge or criticise anyone; and second, we rarely know enough about someone's private life and inner thoughts to be able to make a definitive statement. It can happen that a person who is a believer does not always have faith which is active and operational in every area of his life.

These different areas of life can be likened to various fields. It is only from those fields where seed has been sown that there will be a harvest. If you yourself have fields where you are ignorant of God's will, you will not sow any seed there. The devil will take his opportunity of doing so instead and you will reap a wrong harvest. You may be fully assured about the fact that you are a child of God, but altogether lacking in the knowledge and certainty that God wants to heal your body. You will find it easy to resist the temptation to doubt you are a child of God, but be uncertain of God's will to heal you. Without this knowledge, you cannot pray in faith or reap the harvest God has for you in that particular area.

For this reason, Paul prays that *the God of our Lord Jesus Christ, the Father of glory, may give to you the spirit of wisdom and revelation in the knowledge of Him,* **the eyes of your understanding being** *enlightened; that you may know what is the hope of His calling, what are the riches of the glory of His inheritance in the saints, and what is the exceeding greatness of His power toward us who believe* (Ephesians 1:17-19).

Impediment 3: Unwillingness to Obey

The third impediment to your faith is an unwillingness to obey God. Even if I know God's will, it does not necessarily mean I will obey it. In Romans 1:5 Paul says that his task was to *call people from among all the Gentiles to the obedience that comes from faith* (NIV). Faith involves not only hearing what God says, but obeying it as well. Arguments based on reason and experience may rise up as high strongholds against the Word of God and its revelation. But not before I submit my mind, will, and emotions to the Word of God, and accept that God really means what He says, can I receive His blessing. We never help God by offering Him a load of 'explain-aways' and pious excuses.

Very often under the guise of counselling, people say, "We must be careful not to hurt anyone." But God's truth does not hurt people, it sets them free (John 8:31-32). It is more important not to hurt God by being ashamed of His Word and by constantly doubting and explaining away what He says. The Word of God will stand forever, and His will is a blessing beyond description for all those who obey Him in faith. Rebellion, strife, and opposition to what He has clearly said, however, cannot and will not result in blessing.

Impediment 4: Absence of a Good Confession

The fourth impediment is a lack of positive confession. If you know God's will, yet you persist in speaking what is contrary to it with your mouth, your negative words will release exactly the opposite of His will in your life. Words full of unbelief will give the devil the permission and opportunity he needs to carry out his works, even though you know what God's will is. Make sure that your mouth and the words you speak are in accordance with what is in your heart; then the power of God will be released.

Impediment 5: Lack of Action

The fifth impediment is a lack of action. James 2:26 says that *faith without works is dead*. Even if you have heard the Word and know what Jesus wants, it will be of no benefit to you until you do what He has said. John 14:21 says, *He who has My commandments and keeps them, it is he who loves Me.*

You may have been told all your life that you should witness to non-believers about Jesus. You may read books and attend seminars on evangelism, but not until you actually go out and witness, will the power of God be released to salvation. God makes Himself manifest as you *do the Word*. Many people have been deceived on this issue. They wait on God... and wait and wait. They wait for power... and wait and wait. And while they are waiting, they are singing to themselves, *Be still and know that I am God* (Psalms 46:10).

The devil has stolen the initiative from many, many Christians in this way. He has managed to mark down their ideas and initiatives with objections like, "You aren't mature enough yet," or "You're not quite ready for this yet," or "Be careful that you don't get into the flesh."

We have been still far too long! We have let the devil steal our initiative for far too long! We have waited long enough for God to do something. He *has already done* something. He *has allowed* Jesus to die and be raised from the dead, He *has sent* the Holy Spirit, He *has given* us His promises and our marching orders. He is waiting for us, and has been doing so for a long time. When you take a step of faith on what He has said and trust His ability to perform it, His miracle working power will be released.

It was only when Joshua did what God had told him, marched around the walls of Jericho and blew the trumpet, that the walls fell down—not before. It was only when Abraham obeyed and left Ur of the Chaldeans, that he received what he had been promised. It was only when Moses stretched out his rod, that the Red Sea parted. It was only when Naaman obeyed by dipping himself in the Jordan seven times that he was cured of his leprosy. It was only when the ten lepers were on their way to show themselves to the priests that their leprosy disappeared. It was only when the man with the withered hand stretched it out that he was healed. It was only when the woman with the issue of blood pushed her way through the crowd to touch the garments of Jesus that she was cured. It was only when the servants had filled the waterpots and drew from them as Mary had instructed that the water was turned into wine. She had said: *Whatever He says to you, **do it*** (John 2:5).

Faith is action. If your faith is not followed by deeds, it is dead. If you are standing in faith for God to do a miracle in your life, you must begin to act as though you believe it to be true and adjust your life accordingly. If you act contrary to what you believe, your actions reveal that you are not really trusting that God is going to do something.

Impediment 6: Lack of Perseverance

The sixth impediment to your faith is a lack of perseverance. Time does not exist in the heavenly realms. Everything there is in the present tense, and God is "I am." When you connect with Him in the spirit and hear from Him, you experience eternity.

In this world, however, you live within the confines of time, and what God says does not always happen immediately. Miracles are not always instantaneous, nor are all healings always immediate, but this does not mean to say that they are any less supernatural. When things take time to happen, however, we can easily become impatient and lose heart. This is an area the enemy loves to in. If he cannot stop our miracle from coming, he will at least try to delay it, attempting to make us run out of patience and lose faith. But in Mark 11:24

Jesus says, ...*believe that you **have** received it, and it **will** be yours* (NIV). We have to receive our answer by faith and consider it to be true, a faith fact before it has become a physical fact. Although it may take time to happen, Jesus has promised that it *will* indeed happen.

"But how long will it take?" This kind of question always comes to attack us when we have prayed, together with, "How will it happen? And when will it happen?"

It was some time after Abraham had received the promise that Isaac was actually born. In the meantime he was tempted to try to figure out *how* it would happen. He tried to help God by producing the answer himself using human means. But God does not need any help! Leave the question of when and how up to Him, and simply hold fast to your conviction that it *will* happen.

The devil will do what he can to attack and test your faith to see whether or not it is really a firm *evidence of things not seen*. He will bombard you with doubts and create pictures in your imagination telling you your prayers will never be answered. After some time, impatience sets in and the devil finds his *opportune time* (Luke 4:13 NIV).

This is just what happened to Peter as he walked on the water. Everything was fine at first. He kept his eyes fixed on Jesus and stood on the promise: "Come." Suddenly, however, his circumstances began to look threatening and contradictory. The waves grew larger, the wind stronger, his thoughts whirled around in his head and Peter must have thought, "*How* could this possibly be happening?"

We cannot afford to focus our attention on difficult or contradictory circumstances because they take our attention and faith away from Jesus and His promises. The circumstances are constantly changing. It matters not how dark and threatening they may seem, they are still subject to change. Everything in this world is changing and passing away, and for this reason we should not fix our eyes on what is seen. We do not deny the visible, neither do we accept it as final, but by faith we keep our eyes on the promise.

We fix our eyes on the things which are not seen. For *the things which are seen are temporary, but the things which are not seen are eternal* (2 Corinthians 4:18). This Scripture is referring to heaven itself, as well as to the promises and things of eternal value that have been stored up for us there. These things are to be used here and now, and by seeing them in faith we are able to exercise the patience and perseverance we need to obtain them.

Hebrews 6:12 says, *Imitate those who through faith and patience inherit the promises.* Like faith, patience is a force in your inner man. According to Galatians 5:22, patience is one of the fruits of the spirit which will grow and develop within you. Patience and perseverance work alongside your faith, giving you the strength to keep going without giving up.

Many people get excited about the revelation of a new truth from the Word of God, only to rush off and 'see' whether or not walking in faith really works. You have to walk in faith. It means walking in a conviction regarding the will of God. Only when this conviction is present will you be able to withstand the hardships that come as a result of opposition and attack. You have to pay a price before you can walk. You cannot look back after you have put your hand to the plough; you have to keep on ploughing until the job is done. You cannot afford to become indignant when you find darts being fired at you. Instead, you need to take up the shield of faith, with which you can quench all the fiery darts of the enemy (Ephesians 6:16).

When difficulties arise you cannot afford to feel sorry for yourself and say, "Why does this have to happen to me?" 1 Corinthians 10:13 says, *No temptation* [trial or attack] *has overtaken you except such as is common to man; but God is faithful, who will not allow you to be tempted beyond what you are able.* In other words, *do not think it strange concerning the fiery trial which is to try you* (1 Peter 4:12). Do not be surprised at troubles and attacks. They come to everyone, and are not just unusual occurrences that happen only to you. And when they come, God has given you the ability to stand against them. You will never be tempted, tested or attacked beyond your ability.

And what is your ability? It has nothing to do with your physical strength or will power, nor is it your intellectual or emotional capacity. Your ability is your faith, the faith of your heart, the measure that God has given you, which you must put to use. This is your shield of faith which quenches all the fiery darts of the enemy. With this, you can hold your ground and defeat every attack.

The world is full of attacks and opposition and it is in a state of change. Faith, on the other hand, has the capacity to conquer and overcome the world (1 John 5:4-5), and coupled with patience, it helps you go forth with God, in spite of your circumstances. Hebrews 10:36 says, *For you have need of endurance, so that after you have done the will of God, **you may receive the promise.***

Impediment 7: Lack of Love

The seventh impediment to your faith is a lack of love. Galatians 5:6 says, *For in Christ Jesus neither circumcision nor uncircumcision avails anything, but faith working through love.* Faith is made active, operational, and functional through love. Without love, faith is useless. Irrespective of how much knowledge or will power you may have, without love you will see no results. It is impossible to stand in faith for something and bless God while at the same time cursing your fellow man (see James 3:8-12). If you have trouble receiving an answer to prayer, check to make sure that you are walking in love.

One challenge we face in this area is that our concept of love has often been confused. Being loving has usually meant no more than being generally friendly, kind, well-mannered, and refined, with an all-around pleasant manner. But with such outward kindness and good manners people have been swallowing the most heinous doctrines and faithless teachings, and their pleasant way of being presented has only made them easier to swallow. Love means telling the truth, and the

Word of God is truth. When people nullify what God has said under the guise of love and forgiveness, rebellion and backsliding are the result, regardless of how subtly the error may have been presented.

When an answer to prayer seems to take a long time in coming, the devil wants us to become introspective and full of self-doubt. We might even become so inward-looking that we start to believe that something from deep in our past is the source of our problem. Of course, this may well be the case, but it is far more likely that you are simply neglecting to walk in love in your daily life.

If you pray for revival but speak ill of all those who disagree with you, your answer will never come. If you have personal needs, but persist in slandering an individual every time you get together with your friends, you might as well forget about getting your prayers answered. If you pray for healing and hold feelings of resentment, bitterness, and disappointment towards others, you have to forgive them first.

In Mark 11:25-26, Jesus says,

And whenever you stand praying, if you have anything against anyone, forgive him, that your Father in heaven may also forgive you your trespasses. But if you do not forgive, neither will your Father in heaven forgive your trespasses.

In other words, forgiveness is a condition for answered prayer, while unforgiveness is an impediment. It makes no difference what others may have done to you or how right you are in bearing a grudge. You have to forgive them, anyway. And you *are able* to forgive because *the love of God has been poured out in our hearts by the Holy Spirit who was given to us* (Romans 5:5). God wants you to use the supernatural ability He has given you to love your enemies and forgive those who have wronged you.

To forgive is to forget. This is how God forgives you. He covers over, blots out, and totally forgets your sins. From His perspective, it is as if you had never done anything wrong (Hebrews 10:17).

This is the extent to which God forgives—and He expects you to forgive in the same manner.

Some people forgive merely because they know they have a duty to do so, but they never really forget the wrong done to them. They remember it well and keep a careful account of how others have wronged them. They may be right about the fact that they have been wronged, but they are very wrong in keeping an account of it. They add up the wrongs done to them, meditate over them, and allow disappointment and bitterness find a root in their hearts.

Bitterness and disappointment are amongst the most fatal of all spiritual diseases. They spread like a plague, since people who are full of bitterness never keep it to themselves. They spread slander, ill-feeling, and resentment to all those around them. They search for the weaknesses and faults of the person they are bitter toward and delight in sharing them with anyone who may be available.

This kind of person may even be used by God and may have done great things for Him. Even so, their disappointment has them on the path to spiritual catastrophe and ruin. Psalm 1:1 warns us not to sit *in the seat of the scornful*. Do not do that, because you will become contaminated with their criticism and bitterness. Instead we should *pursue righteousness, faith, love, peace with those who call on the Lord out of a pure heart* (2 Timothy 2:22).

Fellowship with those whose motives are pure and who are not governed by pride, envy, disappointment, bitterness or rebellion. If the people with whom you associate are constantly cutting you down, calling into question what God is doing, and making cynical, disparaging statements, ask God to lead you into better fellowship. Ask Him to lead you to people whose hearts are fervent in spirit, whose mouths are filled with the Word of God and praise, and whose lives are active in serving the Lord rather than in mocking others. This will spare you a lot of misery!

Forgiveness is a one-sided affair. You do it without demanding that the other person ask your forgiveness or change their ways. Instead, be sure to be quick to change when you are wrong. Be sure to be quick to ask for forgiveness, and quick to forgive. In doing so you will keep yourself spiritually healthy, your faith will be active and operational through love, and you can expect to see your prayers answered.

Love is not just loving those who think like you. In Ephesians 1:15 Paul tells the believers that he has heard of their faith and their love for all the saints, not just for those with whom they agreed. We have a responsibility to love every believer, as well as every man and woman on earth.

You have been placed in a particular spot on the wall and you cannot run around like a whirlwind working everywhere, but you can appreciate every one of them, thank God for every one of them and pray for every one of them.

God is doing a great deal in a variety of places, not just where you happen to be. There may be a significant amount of difference between believers, both in doctrine and in practice, but the real question is whether or not they are born again, love Jesus, and desire to obey His commands and carry out the Great Commission. If this is the case, you have much in common with them, and you should be able to love, appreciate, and speak well of them and thank God for what He is doing among them. This will safeguard you in humility and protect you from manipulation and envy.

God will perform miracles wherever He is allowed to. The more we cover one another's shortcomings with love, the greater freedom He will have to operate. If you have received something from God, you have no reason to be proud or boastful. What you have received is there so others can be blessed. What you have is there to help others see Jesus more clearly, and as they do, He will be exalted and glorified and will draw many people to Himself.

Books by Ulf Ekman

A Life of Victory
The guidance, help and inspiration you need to put God's Word first. Fifty-four chapters, each dealing with a particular area of the believer's life. 288 pages.

All Things Are Possible
Thousands of people have been touched by the power of the messages and can testify that their lives have been changed. Now, this teaching is avaiable in published form, through this book. 408 pages.

Another Day of Victory
In this devotional book, Pastor Ulf Ekman enlightens a scripture each dag—from the first day of January to the last day of December. 408 pages.

The Anointing
Ulf Ekman looks at what the anointing is and how it functions. He explains how you can receive the anointing of the Holy Spirit, the various ways in which it is manifested and how to release it in every situation. You can, as a believer, have the same anointing that Jesus had when He lived on this earth!

The Apostolic Ministry
How do we recognise an Apostle? What role does the Apostle have? What can we learn from the life of Paul, the greatest Apostle? Ulf Ekman gives Biblical guidance in this book. 128 pages.

The Authority in the Name of Jesus
When you receive a revelation of what the name of Jesus really means, you will have boldness like never before. Booklet, 32 pages.

The Bible is God's Word
The most important descision you can make once you have been saved is to believe the Bible in its entirety. The Bible is actually the equipment primarily used by God to have fellowship with you, teach you and lead you. Booklet, 32 pages.

Born to win
When you were born, God planned for your success. He created you in His images, to be a bearer of fruit. God is not limited by the opinions of others, and neither are His children. He has determined that you will be successful and bear much fruit. 106 pages.

Call Yourself Blessed
You have the right to call yourself blessed. You are created for blessing, called to be blessed, redeemed so that you can be blessed and you can choose blessing. Booklet, 32 pages.

The Church of the Living God
The Church of the Living God is something far beyond what we think or experience. It is the place where the End-time Revival will have its source and climax—and you have a place in that Church. 158 pages.

Covenant Partner
God has entered into covenant with you through Jesus Christ. That means that He has given Himself to you. Everything He is and has is at your disposal. Booklet, 32 pages.

The Creative Mind
A person will never be greater than he or she thinks. Choose to set your mind on what God has promised and marvel as the power of God is released in your life as your thinking changes. 112 pages.

Destined for Victory
God has victorious plans for you. His plans never fail! In this book you will discover: How to aviod fear of failure, how to withstand the attacks of Satan, how spiritual laws operate and how Gods Word always brings results. Booklet, 32 pages.

Destroy the Works of the Devil
Jesus came to earth to destroy the works of the devil. His death on the cross struck Satan a death blow. Jesus triumphed over him and won the victory for YOU! Booklet, 32 pages.

Faith that Overcomes the World
Explains how faith arises, how it becomes operational, and what makes it grow. 144 pages.

Financial Freedom
A thorough, biblical study on money, riches and material possessions. 128 pages.

The Foundations of our Faith
Ulf Ekman gives an objective and biblical account of each fundamental doctrine of the Christian faith. In days when the Christian message is increasingly diluted and twisted Doctrine will be an asset for every pastor, leader and believer. 256 pages.

God is a Good God
God has given you abundantly more than you can ever grasp for your entire lifetime. This book examines God's character and nature, and reveals His overflowing love for you. Booklet, 32 pages.

God, the State and the Individual
God not only deals with individuals, but with nations and governments. You can change the destiny of your nation! 112 pages.

God Wants to Heal Everyone
Discover the wonderful fact that God's will is to heal everyone—including you. Booklet, 32 pages.

God's Model for Revival
In this booklet, Ulf Ekman emphasises the important role of the church in making believers carriers of revival. If there is true commitment to the vision of the church and to what God is doing, the church will grow and revival will be a fact.
Booklet, 32 pages.

Hearing God's Voice
A lot of people wonder if it is possible to hear what God says. And if it is possible—what required in order to hear His voice? This booklet makes it very clear and uncomplicated. Booklet, 32 pages.

The Highest Purpose
You cannot imagine what a high price Jesus paid for each individual person. You cannot imagine how passionately He loves every single one. It is time for you to come into the highest purpose of your life: to go to the nations. Booklet, 32 pages.

The Holy Spirit
The Holy Spirit is your guide, your teacher, your counselor and your helper. Discover how you can live each day in the power of the Holy Spirit. Booklet, 32 pages.

I Found my Destiny
Follow Ulf Ekman from his boyhood home in Gothenburg to "Livets Ord"—Word of Life Church in Uppsala, Sweden. From 1983 until today Word of Life has become a center for education, evangelism, mission and reformation in Sweden and throughout the world. 150 pages.

Jesus Died for You
Blessing is a daily reality when you understand the power of the cross: Satan's plans were crushed, sickness was defeated, poverty was broken and depression turned to joy. Booklet, 32 pages.

The Jews—People of the Future
Clarifies basic truths about the people and the land. Historical facts and biblical prophecies combine to reveal the fulfillment of God's End-time Plan. 160 pages.

The Lord is a Warrior
In this book, Ulf Ekman explains your victorious position in Christ Jesus and what will happen when you apply all that Jesus has won for you through His atoning sacrifice. 140 pages.

Not Guilty
We often pray for forgiveness for everything we do—even when we are right. This is because we have not understood teaching on righteousness, which frees us to be ourselves, to be the people we really are. Booklets, 32 pages.

Prayer Changes Nations
Ulf Ekman teaches here on what characterizes the time before revival, the work that needs to be done and how the Holy Spirit can change every believer into a bold prayer-warrior. 156 pages.

Prayer That Changes Things
Prayer becomes a special joy when you realise that it does not mean rattling off a list of requests or fullfilling religious duties, but that it is fellowship with the Living God—every day. Booklet, 32 pages.

The Power in the New Creation
A new dimension of victorious living awaits you. The Lord is with you, Mighty Warrior! Booklet, 32 pages.

The Prophetic Ministry
"Provides essential guideposts for the operation of the prophetic ministry today." From the Foreword by Demos Shakarian. 224 pages.

Your Capacity on God
The book teaches you to understand and release God's possibilities that are already stored up inside of you. You can reach the full potential of what God has invested in you! 153 pages.

What Faith Is
Faith is very simply accepting what God has already carried out for you through Jesus Christ. This booklet addresses what is perhaps the most important subject in the Bible-faith. Booklet, 32 pages.

When the World is Shaken
A terrible act of terror occurred in the USA on September 11, 2001. The war against terrorism, whether it is from Muslim fundamentalists or not, will cause the world to become colder and harder. Booklet, 32 pages.

Available from your local Christian bookstore, or order direct from the publisher:

Sweden: Word of Life Publications
P.O. Box 17, S-751 03, Uppsala, Sweden. Telephone +46 18 16 14 30
Fax +46 18 69 31 90. E-mail order@livetsord.se
Australia: Ulf Ekman Ministries
P.O. Box 2324 Mansfield Qld. 4122.
Telephone/fax +61 73 849 53 25.
E-mail australia@ulfekman.org

UK: Word of Life Sweden
P.O. Box 70, Edenbridge, Kent TN8 5ZG UK.
Telephone +44 1732 86 71 71
Fax +44 1732 86 71 11. E-mail uk@ulfekman.org
USA/Canada: Ulf Ekman Ministries
P.O. Box 700717, Tulsa, OK 74170, USA. Telephone +1 714 374 6806
Toll free # 1 800 428 1760. E-mail usa@ulfekman.org